MY LIFE AS LAURA

MY LIFE AS LAURA

How I Searched for Laura Ingalls Wilder and Found Myself

KELLY KATHLEEN FERGUSON

PRESS 53
Winston-Salem

Press 53
PO Box 30314
Winston-Salem, NC 27130

First Edition

Cover design by Kevin Morgan Watson

Map Copyright © 2011by Catherine Chamis

Library of Congress Control Number: 2011916071

Printed on acid-free paper
ISBN 978-1-935708-44-5

For Mom,
who knew exactly which books to give
her daughter on her sixth birthday

CONTENTS

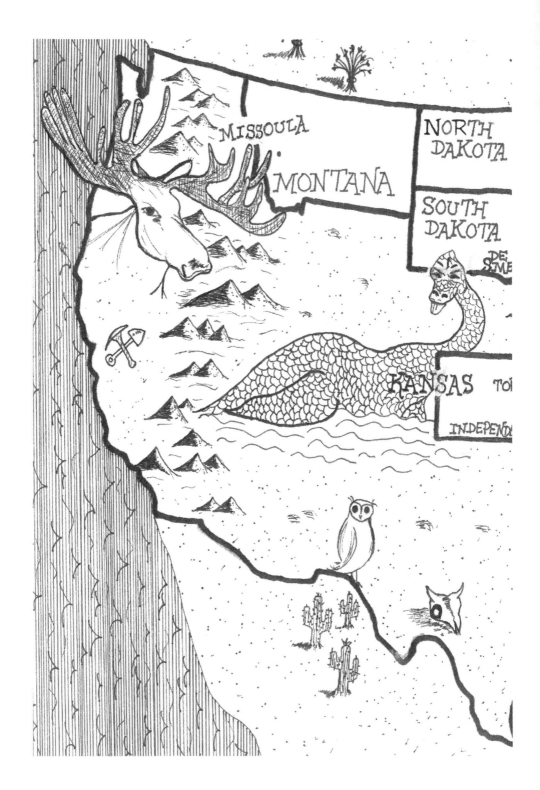

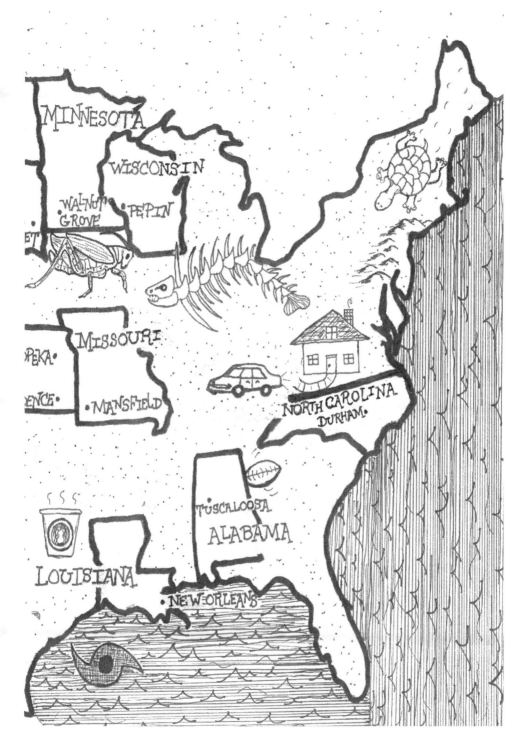

CHAPTER ONE
WOMANIFEST DESTINY

Tuscaloosa, Alabama
Durham, North Carolina
Missoula, Montana

I admit that the origin of the dress mandate was fuzzy at best. All I can say is the instant I decided to retrace the pioneer journey of Laura Ingalls Wilder, I knew I would wear a Laura dress. When I first envisioned this costume, my intention had been to browse online, haunt thrift stores, contact a seamstress, research historical garb, etc. What happened: I was leaving the next day and needed a dress.

That afternoon I scouted the local Goodwill, hoping for a miracle in the racks. Nope. I resigned myself to a vintage shop. As a general rule I dislike shopping in a place where a bored employee has nothing to do but stare me down. Help galls me, as I possess a toddlerlike insistence that *I can do it myself.* A poorling, I do not belong in the specialty spending bracket, and I hate telling people no, so I rank boutique shopping on the comfort par of wool sheets. Waiting until the final hour, I barreled into Mr. Higgins' Vintage Clothing & Costumes of Missoula, Montana, all bluster and little intention.

Which explains why I was unprepared for this challenge posed by the owner.

"Do you want to dress like Laura the little *girl,*" she asked, scrunching up her face and tilting her head, "or Laura the adult?"

The proprietor folded antique bandannas on a display case while

I processed. She looked somewhere between forty and eighty, youthful despite the crinkles. I had met her type a few times now, the western woman who could charge an alpine escarpment, dragging her giant dog while I clutched a scrubby tree and panted. Her unexpected question, and inescapable inflection, made me realize that a thirty-eight-year-old woman dressing like a little pioneer girl was odd. And not odd in a quirky, adorable way, but odd in a *Whatever Happened to Baby Jane* way.

I inhaled the aroma of antique, steam-pressed sweat and rolled the dilemma around on my tongue, as though contemplating a flavor. This Laura dress issue was getting complicated. A basic getup began with the red calico worn by little girl Laura, but as Laura became a young woman, her wardrobe expanded. Passages detail her outfits—the brown poplin with her ostrich-feathered poke bonnet, her pink lawn, the black cashmere that became her wedding dress, but even if I chose an "adult" Laura dress, I would only be fifteen. At my age the real Laura was a farmer's wife in Mansfield, and those clothes were not part of the Books.

To my relief, the owner had not asked *why* I needed a Laura dress, a question way too involved for me to answer right then. She didn't even blink. As it turned out, my request was routine—in Missoula, Montana, people needed Laura dresses all the time. There were Frontier Days, reenactments of homestead life, and you never knew when Hellgate High might rally for another production of *Oklahoma!* The more we discussed options, I found myself grateful for professional help. A prairie newbie, I had not considered that I would need a bonnet and apron, or even known that the nineteenth-century style was Victorian. The owner said she was usually buried in calico and gingham, except she had just made a huge donation to the historical society.

Yesterday.

We leafed through her back stock of cowgirl outfits and flapper dresses with fringe. When I saw the rack of clown costumes, I began to panic a little. After an extensive search, we were able to roust out three dresses remotely suitable, not one of them a red calico or brown poplin with an ostrich-feathered poke bonnet. I took my options into the dressing room and drew the flowered curtain.

Number One was a tiny yellow calico that had the girth of a sock. Number Two, brown with vanilla piping, looked doubtful (size and style-wise), but I tried anyway. It reached an impasse at my knees. I remembered yet another reason why I dislike vintage clothing stores: nothing ever fits.

I confronted Number Three, my last chance—the floor-length, turquoise-blue-flowered dress with a scooped neck trimmed in ribbon and lace, cap sleeves, and a fluorescent-orange dust ruffle. Blue was Mary's color, not Laura's, but I rationalized that Laura had always wished she could wear blue. I chanted Laura's mantra when facing the unavoidable—it couldn't be helped.

In the end, the primary selling point of the blue dress was this: it zipped.

So, why did I need a Laura dress?

The origins of my pioneer story began October 2, 1974, in a little house made of red brick in Tuscaloosa, Alabama. On that day my mother gave me the Laura Ingalls Wilder box set for my sixth birthday, the yellow-covered Harper Trophy Edition illustrated by Garth Williams. I don't know what the set cost, but individual books retailed for $1.50 ($1.70 Canada). At some point I took a magic marker and wrote my name in the space provided (*Belongs to* _____), scribing each letter with extreme focus. This was serious business.

From first read, I absorbed the story of Laura and her family's nineteenth-century pioneer journey west as my own, and I became determined to live like my idol. It wasn't easy, proving up a claim in the twentieth-century suburbs, but I applied my homesteader work ethic. I built cabins out of Lincoln Logs and tended faithfully to my plastic mustangs. Autumn I gathered acorns and dried Kudzu berries on the back deck. Winter I braided pine straw to burn in the fireplace, watching with satisfaction as my fuel turned blue, then white, then withered into smoke up the flue, tossing in tiny log after log, until my parents asked me to *please stop that*. Spring I plowed the centipede grass, cursing those pesky roots. Summer I sowed birdseed crops in the houseplants that my mom, sighing, yanked out. With the tenacity

3

of Charles Ingalls, I dutifully replanted despite the destructive forces of nature.

Plant, milk, bake, sew, churn—Laura always got the job done. I puttered my Big Wheel around the cul-de-sac, a life devoid of action verbs. Clearly, I was living in the wrong century, with the wrong family. Our pantry was stuffed with a cornucopia of Fudge Deelites, Little Debbie Swiss Cakes, Nutter Butters and Chips Ahoy, but I read with fascination about Laura's Ma who brought out a tiny bag of sugar for company, carefully doling out the granules. Not to be outdone, I rationed my M&M's, denying myself the green ones for minutes at a time.

Laura inspired me to think about how others experience the world. In homage to her blind sister, Mary, I practiced sitting happily alone in the corner and learned to "see with my fingers," sorting my stuffed animals by feel. Eyes closed, I galumphed around the house until I banged into a piece of furniture.

"Goldangit!" I yelped.

"Can't you find something to do?" my parents asked.

On the surface I had more than enough to do, a fact Mom and Dad liked to point out as I whined, dragging my feet on the shag carpet. I had TV: *Gilligan's Island*, *The Brady Bunch*, *My Three Sons* and *I Dream of Jeannie*. I had games: Wiffle balls, Lemon Twists, Quick Curl Barbies and Games of Life. I had activities: swim team, jazz tap, conversational Spanish, piano lessons, gymnastics, macramé, charm school, Girl Scouts, calligraphy, orienteering, stamp collecting, birding, baton twirling and backyard astronomy. In short, I could whip out a yarn and popsicle stick God's eye like nobody's business.

My number one complaint?

"I'm bored."

My mother's response was to give me a task, but dusting knickknacks was not the same as planting the wheat crop. Our family's survival did not depend on whether the Hummel plates gleamed to perfection, and my craft projects only generated more dust. I was unneeded—worse—a drain. The only hope was I would become a doctor one day and take my parents on trips to Italy. In the meantime, I was told to be grateful, to which I gave the age-old retort, "I didn't ask to be born."

4

I best helped my family by leaving them alone and reading in my room, so that's what I did. I splayed my body like a starfish on the pink frilly bedspread surrounded by white princess furniture. There, as Laura, I relived my past life as Pa's right-hand girl. We forged bullets to protect the home and provide meat for the family. We built a door on the log cabin in the Indian Territory. We made hay while the Dakota sun shone. Pa said time and again how he didn't know what he'd do without his Half-Pint. Without me, everyone would have died, their bones picked over by wolves and turned to dust on the high prairie.

Kelly was an annoying kid in everyone's way, but Kelly as Laura mattered.

The next chapter in this story takes place twenty-five years later, in a little blue house with green shutters in Durham, North Carolina.

At this time I had been in Durham for sixteen years and in the same house for more than a decade. For work, I had waited tables since college. This meant I had been asking people if they would care for more coffee since the summer of my sophomore year, with that first job at a Shoney's Big Boy.

Regularly, customers (okay, senior citizens struggling with atmospheric lighting) would ask, "Are you a student? What's your major?"

Why yes, I was a student of literature and philosophy at the University of North Carolina at Chapel Hill. Sixteen years ago. Care to discuss Albert Camus, the Myth of Sisyphus and the only true question of suicide? How's your chicken?

Back in my philosophy days, I studied Heraclites, the ancient Greek who made the claim that no man steps in the same river twice, for it's not the same river and he's not the same man. For years I had stood in the same river thinking I could defeat change, but what I discovered is that even if you stay put, the river changes around you. Years elapse and there you are, waterlogged and shivering, wondering where the party went. It seemed everyone I knew had passed me by. Maybe they moved to Seattle, San Francisco or New York. Maybe they were married with children. Maybe they established meaningful careers. I wasn't jealous of anyone in particular, but I was very jealous of everyone in general. I felt as though I had never grown up.

Change is difficult for me. I have always been, as they say, a bit touched. I interpret even minor setbacks—parking tickets or flat soda—as a personal message from the Universe. *Dear Kelly, I hate you. The Universe.* Now all my fear and indecision over small problems had added up to one real dilemma—I was stuck. Not only had my twenties flown by, my thirties were in serious jeopardy.

When times were hard, my escape since childhood had always been reading, but these days I couldn't face adult literary fiction. I didn't have the strength for Oprah Book Club stories of child abuse, Russian novels or self-conscious narratives about our postmodern condition. I tried reading so-called escape books, romance novels and chick lit, but these functioned like a backhanded compliment or junk food—a brief surge of pleasure before the crash and a yucky feeling deep inside.

Those stories were fake.

Then I saw the yellow box set.

Ever since a brief separation in college, the yellow box set— the same yellow box set from my childhood—had been with me, but sat unread on the bookshelf. The keepsake conjured fond memories, but I wasn't sure I cared to relive my childhood pioneer days any more than I wished to macramé an owl plant hanger or watch *The Bionic Man*. There's a danger in looking up past loves. It's usually best to keep sacred memories sacred, or they are bound to disappoint. As a kid I cherished Hostess cupcakes; now they taste like wax. I once admired fuzzy carpet toilet seat covers and American eagle lamps. My favorite song in fourth grade was "Undercover Angel, Midnight Fantasy." Enough said. If Laura wasn't going to hold up, I didn't want to know, but on this day, as though guided by a latent muscle memory, my marionette hand reached for the Books.

I re-creased the binding of *Little House in the Big Woods* and was greeted by an orange Kraft Macaroni and Cheese stain.

Once upon a time, sixty years ago, a little girl lived in the Big Woods of Wisconsin in a little gray house made of logs.

I crawled in bed and read under the covers. By page two I was consumed by the desire to roast a pig's tail, practically able to lick that hot, crackling fat off my fingers. I raced to reach the sugaring off dance at Grandma's, filled with a desperate yearning to read the sentence that described Aunt Docia's juicy blackberry buttons.

Clarence the naughty cousin. Ma's butter pats with the tiny strawberry leaves. Angels in the snow. They had been waiting for me, suspended in time. I don't know that I exhaled until I reached the final scene of the Ingalls family gathered 'round while Pa played his fiddle. As soon as I finished the first book I reached for the next, and the next, and the next. I devoured the series, rediscovering the many tiny miracles: Mr. Edwards, the wildcat from Tennessee; Jack, the loyal bulldog; Ma's vanity cakes—each detail like finding an Easter egg.

And here's what happened: The more I read about Laura's life, the more I was able to connect with my own. Once again I knew right from wrong, friend from enemy. I marveled at the huge blue sky and savored each bite of meat. Laura understood my struggles to be good—and my lapses. She got that I could enjoy sports and love girly clothes. Through Laura I reconnected with my ambition: there was nothing wrong with wanting to be the best. The pell-mell of my addled brain settled out. I returned to center. I could deal.

And I remembered.

Kelly didn't always know what to do, but Kelly as Laura did.

Laura was back in my life, just as though she had never left. From then on, whenever I was confused or down, I turned to the Books, and they set me straight.

One evening, I was reading *By the Shores of Silver Lake* on the front porch swing of my little blue house. A huge oak stood across the street, with branches like giant arteries in the sky. I slouched sideways, pressed my foot against the swing's metal chain, let go and swayed, and read, and stared at the tree. And it was while staring at the oak tree, reading about Laura riding black ponies across the prairie, that I knew what I wanted. Or rather, drawing upon Laura's strength, I wasn't afraid to know what I wanted, and what I wanted was a change. It was time to stop writing in my journal about wanting to move, or if I should move, or where should I move, and move.

With Laura as my guide, naturally, I would go west.

West.

How had I never thought of it before? I had always been Pa's girl, eyes fixed on the setting sun. After twenty years of wanting to "do something," this was it. I was wrenching free of the tar baby, busting out of the cul-de-sac, dislodging the mental wagon wheel mired in mud. After some deliberation, but not so much I lost my nerve, I decided on the destination of Missoula, Montana. Once decided, I decided to be decided, before I talked myself out of risking as I had so many times before. Like a kid rechecking a Christmas list for Santa, I would get out my map and contemplate this previously unconsidered, enormous state near Canada.

Looks cold, I thought.

"Montana!" my friends gasped. "Maybe you'll meet yourself a cowboy!"

Despite the allure of straight men in chaps, it took months to extract myself from the spider web of my former life. The South does not release her subjects easily. Beyond the emotional entanglements, I had to empty the house, which meant sorting through two decades of gathered belongings. There is no need to dwell here as I suspect these details could grow tiresome, but I offer these tidbits: (1) there was a piano; (2) there was a shed. Those last weeks I lifted so many boxes my biceps visibly developed, but finally, finally, finally I hauled the last load to my Toyota Camry, freshly outfitted with new tires and an oil change.

Done.

Before getting in the car, I turned and studied the little blue house that had absorbed over a decade of my prime. I thought of weekends lost questing for the right bathroom fixture, screw or slab of antique wood siding. People talk about how a third of our life is spent sleeping, I had spent at least that wandering the aisles of Home Depot. I admired the paint job. Just a few months ago, I had agonized over the exterior color, night after night falling asleep in a pile of paint chips, ruminating—what if I pay $4,000 to make my house Denim Azure, and then *I don't like it?* As it turned out, the color was perfect, but I had been asking myself the wrong question.

I got in my car, pulled the door shut.

The trip odometer rolled at 1,800 miles as I entered South Dakota. At this point North Carolina, Tennessee, Illinois, Missouri and Iowa were behind me. The initial thrill had settled into a flat pink rim around my eyes. My mouth had the permanent taste of fast food acid reflux and my butt the texture of an old sponge. I was in the doldrums, which is why I was caught unprepared as I pulled over to pump my umpteenth tank of gas.

North of Iowa the sea level rises gradually, and the barometric pressure changes. I stepped out, emerging from the humidity basin reborn. I felt different, lighter, that tingly feeling before a storm. My body was standing still, but it was as though the gliding motion of the car remained with me. I gazed out on the swell of unbroken prairie to the west. The endless gray hills were like the moon and about as foreign. My eyes had no tree to grip, giving me a slight sense of vertigo. The unfettered wind ran wild as it pleased. In a second, the light film of sweat I had worn my entire life vanished.

West began.

A Native American woman rang up my trough-sized Coke. Charged, I sprang back to the car, pumped full of adrenaline. One hit and I was a western landscape junkie, desperate to maintain my high. The long, flat highway beckoned. I lapped up the mile markers, one after another in rapid succession. I began to speed, pushing the red needle 80… 85… 90… I was Wonder Woman flying her invisible jet, rushing to save the day.

Then, at 6:30 p.m., forty-eight miles past Sioux Falls, I encountered a Sign.

Laura Ingalls Wilder Homestead. Exit 271.

BRAKES.

The Camry lurched, and my giant drink sloshed forward in a tidal wave. If there were anything to hit in South Dakota, I would have wrecked the car. I was six again and victim to the maddening tinkle of the ice cream truck. The same sense of sheer panic

9

hijacked my thoughts as they squirreled back and forth. *Should I flag the truck down? Or run inside and ask for money first?* For the first time in years I had that childhood sense that if I didn't get what I wanted, *I would die.*

As it was, some puckerbrush received a little impromptu landscaping before I swerved back on the road. Reality: I wasn't a kid chasing an ice cream truck, and a U-turn right then was out of the question. Adult concerns, such as employment and housing issues, waited west of the continental divide. Before I knew it, the Sign was behind me, a flash in the rearview mirror that dimmed before fading away. Soon the lull of I-90 closed the fabric tear in the universe. My heartbeat settled, and I convinced myself I was grown-up now, everything was okay. In Mitchell, South Dakota, I received a sobering $125 speeding ticket. The eternal vista of prairie, groundhog villages and SEE WALL DRUG signs eroded my emotional state back down to a mature flavor of monotony.

Except a tiny piece of my six-year-old heart remained at Exit 271. The Sign was bookmarked in my mind, like a Little Debbie wrapper holding my place in *Little Town on the Prairie.*

Montana fulfilled my starry-eyed expectations. A river ran through it, rugged and improbable as any dream. I belted whisky with grizzled men in outpost watering holes. There were osprey and moose. I gripped tin cups of coffee and shouted, "Yar!" at the snowy peaks. I even met my cowboy in the form of an information technology whisperer/poet. We forged a romance, our bodies pressed against a keno machine at the Silver Dollar Bar.

But if I was a frontier woman on the outside, inside I remained the suburban Jell-O mold that never took—still wobbly after all these years.

And I knew who could help.

The bracing air had activated my pioneer spirit, the Sign pulsing in my chest, a siren song. I had seen one, so there must be others. I searched my atlas for Laura's little towns on the prairie. These places had always seemed exotic to me; I suppose I never thought of them as real. It was shocking to see these holy sites marked by tiny black dots on a map. Pepin. Walnut Grove. De Smet. Laura's pioneer journey west had not taken place in a galaxy far, far away. It could be plotted on a AAA Trip Tik and connected by an orange highlighter.

It was while staring at this map that a plot tumbled out of my mind like an unexpected child—a bit daunting, but impossible to put back. My scheme was this: I would travel west from the Big Woods of Pepin, Wisconsin, to the Great Plains of De Smet, South Dakota, and as I retraced the physical path of Laura's coming of age, I would relive and rebuild my own.

I had two weeks, five towns, my yellow box set and a bright blue dress. With Laura as my guide, this time I would get it right.

CHAPTER TWO
IN WHICH ISSUES ARE A DRESS(ED)

Pepin, Wisconsin: *Little House in the Big Woods*

Room One of the Lake Pepin Inn was plain, but clean and comfortable with dark carpet, maple furnishings, and twig wreaths on the pale walls. It was drizzly outside in a cool and easy way. From my window, I could see the Pepin Historical Museum across the street. The false front featured the wooden silhouette of a pioneer girl in a country blue dress with a white bonnet that hid her face like a monk's hood. A rainbow kite waved, "OPEN."

I took out a notebook and pen and wrote:

To Do
Laura Ingalls Wilder Museum
Pepin Tourist Information
Little House Wayside

It had taken me almost a year to get here, as my scheme had to lie fallow until the following summer. Winter isn't road trip season in states that border Canada, and funds had to be gathered. Like farmers in the off season, I laid the groundwork for busier times ahead. By July I had my itinerary and was ready to roll. In my trip research, I discovered Laurafans before me had been hard at work; each homesite had historic and tourist attractions. There were replica log cabins, restored historical buildings, museums, tombstones, celebratory pageants and commemorative plaques. I would see them all. I ruled out travel to Malone, New York, the homesite of *Farmer Boy* (Almanzo's childhood story), as I eliminated peripheral sites involving the Ingalls family. My focus would remain on Laura's pioneer journey, as written about in the Books. The exception to this rule would be a final stop in Mansfield, Missouri, where Laura farmed, wrote the Books and lived into old age.

Circumstances were unfortunate in that since I now lived in Montana, I had to "backtrail" East. This went sorely against my frontierswoman instincts, as backtrailing in the nineteenth century was tantamount to failure. I wished I could beam like a Star Trek crew member or *tesseract* like Meg Murry from *A Wrinkle in Time*. Regrettably, my transport was the workaday Toyota Camry, although I took solace in the superior gas mileage and consistently high ratings in *Consumer Reports*. To minimize the backtrail effect, I blitzed eastward north of all Laura towns and took as much interstate as possible, which has a way of neutralizing location. Once in Pepin, I solemnly declared pioneer do-over. To herald my rebirth, I would don my Laura dress for the first time, which I would then wear for the entire trip.

From the instant I hatched my scheme, I had talked up my dress and my trip to anyone and everyone in range.

Person in Search of Idle Conversation: "Hey, what's up?"

Me: "I'm going to retrace the pioneer journey of Laura Ingalls Wilder. In a Laura dress."

In this moment I gave my best Holden Caulfield shrug, as though last year I climbed the *Crime and Punishment* staircase in period costume and planned on scaling Mount Fuji in a sumo thong the next. People were impressed by my adventurous spirit, wowed by my quirky savoir faire, or at least they were very, very polite.

"That's so brave!" they cried.

"That's hilarious!" they laughed.

"You're what?" queried the confused.

"You always did like those books," said my mother.

Some people had no idea who Laura Ingalls Wilder was, and those people did not count.

"Wasn't there that television show?" they asked.

"Never mind," I said.

Talk is one thing, I believe *cheap* would be the word. Now I had to make good on my boast. Just as *Big Woods* is a relatively simple tale of little pioneer girl and her family, my goals for this first stop were pretty modest—work up the nerve to walk outside in this dress.

With the moment of reckoning upon me, I sat on the bed and examined my impulse buy with more scrutiny, mesmerizing myself on the buds and mossy green leaves until I discovered an array of tiny black circles, like pond life. The blue was more suited to a Carolina Tar Heel than a Victorian-era homesteader, and the print was not the least nineteenth century. So far as I could tell, the pattern belonged to no century, yet neither could I describe it as timeless. The ribbon and lace seemed silly, and the orange flounce could stop traffic.

The more I stared at this big blue monster in my closet, the more I realized that wearing a Laura dress would be more stressful than travel as a regular tourist. People might think I was delusional, an escapee from a fundamentalist religious compound, or A Cry for Help. I had no idea how they might react, but no matter what, there could be no hiding. I would be noticed. In all my years of restaurant work, I never got over that flinch of nerves as I approached a table. Ever. I had been foolish to believe I could romp around the Midwest in a kooky costume without my old friend social anxiety hitching a ride. I flashed back to the wary, doubtful reaction of the Mr. Higgins' Vintage Clothing & Costumes proprietor. Brave and hilarious were descriptions I enjoyed. Desperate and psychologically warped? Not so much.

I could just skip the dress, I rationalized. *It wasn't as if anyone would know.*

Except the yellow box on the handcrafted Amish desk.

I finished my morning coffee and read a bit. I touched my toes and cranked out a few karate kicks. Maybe I should call my parents sometime soon; I was a lousy daughter and should reach out more. The water faucets turned on and off quite efficiently, I discovered. Good to know. I put ice in a bucket and observed how the ice, in a feat of science, melted. I tested out the Amish rocking chair, marveling over the simplicity and comfort for precisely thirty seconds before I jumped up again. I gnawed an old bagel, something I never would have done in the presence of company, and you know, that bagel made me a little bit sad.

To my credit, I did not turn on the TV, aware that I would get sucked into a *Law and Order* marathon. For while we live in an uncertain world, one constant is that no matter the time of day, or part of the country, *Law and Order* will be on. All it takes is one signature *chong!* for the wheels of justice to hit and run roughshod over my willpower. I could just see my trip devolving into the plotline of "The Trouble with Tribbles"—one seemingly harmless episode quickly multiplying beyond my control. I would regress into a hunched Howard Hughes figure, my yellowed fingernails curling into my forearm, opening the door only for more milk bottles to drink and pee into.

I threw the remote in the nightstand drawer and took one last look at the yellow box.

"It couldn't be helped."

I began the gymnastic routine required to get in the dress, like a prizefighter performing his warm-up exercises. While the dress did (eventually) zip, the procedure required a sharp intake of the breath, a yogic chant (Ohm, Shanti) and a little hop dance to make the metal teeth meet. Help, I discovered, is nice to have sometimes. Like gnawing a stale bagel, zipping a dress that's too tight alone in a hotel room has a depressing effect. Whenever Grace Kelly dressed for a cocktail party, Cary Grant was there. Here I was Wilma without Fred, Ma without Pa, but in true Laura style, I persevered.

Once fastened, the tightness produced a little roll of fat (O! Vanity!) and squeezed my breasts (O! Ashley!) up over the top of the scoop neck in a distinctly *un*-Victorian manner. I braided my hair into pigtails and checked out the final effect—the original St. Pauli Girl prairie hooker. I was appropriately dressed to stand on the corner of a log cabin and greet visitors—"Hey, John, you like to party?"

Of course, I could have skipped the dress. Most people understand that just because you say you are going to do something, doesn't mean you have to actually do it. In Pepin, Wisconsin, hundreds of miles from anyone I knew, I had no witnesses. I had signed no Satanic contracts in blood. I could have bailed. I learned about bailing fifteen years ago from a Californian named Will, who said, "Sometimes you just gotta say, 'Dude, I'm bailing.'" This direct and honest approach has long struck me as a credo to be admired. If only we all conducted our exits with such integrity and grace.

My problem is that I have a long history of sticking out projects any sane person would quit. Take, for example, my (basically) random decision at twenty-three to be a rock drummer. Drums are loud. Drums are heavy. Drums take time to set up and break down. Drums are also hard to play. If I wanted to be in a band, I could have played bass. Basic rock bass is relatively easy, but no way would I play bass because I had determined that chick bass players were cliché. I got this idea in my head that I didn't want to play "the girlfriend instrument," even though I discovered tragically late in the game that I was a natural bass player, with a left hand that wrapped around the fret like a hug. But stubborn me wouldn't switch instruments. Oh, no, no, no. For years I endured band meetings where we discussed What To Do About Kelly. Eventually, with diligence and lessons and tears and a decade of experience, I got pretty good.

Then the band broke up.

I emerged from my music career middle-aged and in debt, and my next book will be a memoir/tome called *What Was I Thinking?*

One more story:

The Day I Learned Kermit the Frog's Job Is Hard

When I was perhaps nine, I read a book about a girl who put on a puppet show for the neighborhood and made enough money to purchase a bicycle, which struck me as about the most brilliant scheme ever. I pestered my mother into inviting all the neighborhood kids and their mothers. I set up chairs and made a stage by hanging a sheet over a jump rope spanned between two chairs. I gathered my puppets (Baby Alive head, Malibu Barbie, Ernie, all my stuffed animals) and colored a huge sign proclaiming the price of admission. (I wanted to charge ten dollars—my mother talked me down to a quarter.)

All this was great fun, but really, after coloring the sign, I was done. Imagine my shock when an actual audience arrived. Showtime, I hid behind the sheet with my cast and came to the terrible realization that I had taken care of every detail except one—a script. In short, I had puppets and a puppet stage, but no *puppet show.*

Any sensible kid would have locked herself in the bathroom, feigned illness and refused to perform. Not me. I had said I would put on a puppet show, *so I was going to put on a puppet show.*

Act I: the audience watched a quivering sheet.

After a long, painful pause some kid whined, "I can't seeeeee anything."

Act II: I flung puppets in the air and muttered.

The reviews rolled in.

"Can we go home now?"

"This is stupid."

Yet I kept mumbling and flinging puppets until my mother snuck her head behind the sheet and whispered, "I think you can go ahead and finish up now."

Act III: I hurled the puppets one by one over the sheet into the audience.

Coda: I ran and locked myself in the bathroom, no longer having to feign illness.

Say a person mentions that we should have lunch sometime the following week; I take that as an oath. I'm not saying I have never gone back on a lunch date, that would be silly, but I am saying that if I do, I will feel guilty. I can't cancel a dentist appointment without feeling bad. I can torture myself over a thought promise that I never made out loud. I can mull over a look I gave that relayed an implied promise, or fret over a promise I maybe should have implied but didn't, and in case you were wondering, yes, my family background is Roman Catholic.

Bailing wasn't in my character.

I said I would wear a prairie dress, and so I was going to wear a prairie dress. I might as well get to it.

I girded up my loins and stepped outside, half-expecting Willie Oleson to jump out and yell, "Long-legged snipes!" but all I saw was the desk clerk of the Lake Pepin Inn glance up from her paper, blink once, and look right back down. I would learn this about Midwesterners: They might live in a town with a Subway, one gas station and an old barrel, but that doesn't mean they are easily impressed.

The museum was loosely set up to resemble the Pepin store of *Little House in the Big Woods*. Inventory had changed with the times. Instead of bolts of calico and barrels of corn meal, there were "Pa's Fiddle" magnets, postcard trees and Laura bobblehead dolls, although I did see horehound candy available for the authenticity sticklers. Period artifacts were on display, including an antique cash register and a furnished bedroom. Nineteenth-century tools covered a wall—meat saw, meat hook, bung auger, scythe, hay knife, cross cut saw—giant, rusty instruments that made the average pioneer look like Torquemada of the Plains.

I spied a rack of homemade aprons and bonnets for sale, garments I needed as Mr. Higgins' Vintage Clothing & Costumes had been out. Not only would these accessories provide the kiss of authenticity, an apron would cover up my bosoms and work as a waist slimmer. Excellent. A bonnet was paramount as well, if only to neglect wearing it. I flipped though the selection. The calico print sets available would clash with the wild blue floral print. I was blaming myself once more for being a lousy planner when I found one country white apron and bonnet set. Bone white would have been ideal, but this was much better than forest green with mauve rosebuds. After a bit more nervous browsing, I purchased: *Laura: The Life of Laura Ingalls Wilder, Author of the Little House on the Prairie* by Donald Zochert, a Laura bookmark, and a piece of horehound candy that I later sucked very carefully to make it last.

I emboldened myself to meet the cashier in my first interaction as "Laura." She was also in a prairie dress, but a subdued earth-colored number. I paused to take in the gravity of this moment—first contact with another of my kind. Casually, I placed my purchases on the counter. I had no idea how she would react. Would she hand me a crocheted afghan and tell me to cover myself? She might want to hear about my failed puppet show, or my addiction to *Law and*

Order. Perhaps after a little LIW heart-to-heart she'd invite me out to her lakeside cottage so we could bake dried apple pie in a pattypan.

Cashier (woman with frizzy white hair and heavy-lidded eyes, as if waking up from nap): "Is that all?"

Me: "Yes."

Cashier: "Debit or credit?"

Me: "Debit. Oh, wait. Can I have this postcard, too?"

Cashier: "That'll be $67.53."

Me: "…"

Cashier: "Did you need something else?"

Me: "No."

The tourist center next door had the typical pioneer displays (rifles, skillets, oxbows) and a tower of pamphlets. I did my best to appear "Laura-like," which in my mind meant stoic yet kind and poised for action. A guide was there to explain that yes, indeed, Pepin was the birthplace of the author Laura Ingalls Wilder. I wasn't sure what to say. It seemed silly to ask the Obvious Question as my big flowered dress revealed I knew the answer. But I had the southerner's need for small talk, so I tried.

Interaction Number 2 as Laura:

"Sooooo, this is Pepin."

"Yes, this is the town where Laura Ingalls Wilder was born. Please take a pamphlet."

The woman seemed disappointed that she didn't have more to report. The strain of repeating the same sentence all day weighed heavily on her brow, and I was sorry to have contributed to her suffering. I had already grabbed a stack of pamphlets, but when she handed me another one, I took it.

I retreated to my car, immediately exhaling in relief. I had spent many hours in my tiny gray fortress lately and grown a bit xenophobic as a result. I was beginning to understand Laura's psychological sufferings every time she had a first day of school. When you spend a great deal of time in a confined space with the same people (or in my case alone), strangers become a bit terrifying. I glanced at the clock. All told, my adventures logged in at twenty-three minutes.

A pamphlet let me know that Little House Wayside was located north of Pepin, about fourteen miles down County Road CC. In 1961 the local library committee determined the location of the original Ingalls homestead, but the original cabin had collapsed in the 1920s. The owners of the land donated enough space to build a replica.

> We trust that all who come to Pepin through the inspiration of Laura's books will visit Laura Ingalls Wilder Park in the Village, Little House Wayside at the site of her birth, and the Pepin Historical Museum. It may not be what you expect, but as Laura said, "Now is now, it can never be a long time ago."

As I wove down County Road CC, passing farmhouses and silos, I saw what the pamphlet meant. Laura's Big Woods of elm, oak, ash, maple, basswood, butternut and birch were long gone. The trees (for lumber and, later, to supply the paper industry) had been sacrificed for the Wisconsin economy. Areas such as Pepin were cut first, since the nearby Mississippi made for handy shipping. Entire forests were sent downriver, and in the decade of Laura's birth, the number of board feet shipped from Pepin surged from 60 to 436 million. Laura describes in *Big Woods* how she and her cousins would play by jumping from stump to stump.

Since then, a few trees had sprouted in place, but they would need a few hundred years to create a canopy. I later heard that northern Wisconsin was densely forested, but the County Road CC landscape consisted of farmland. The wolves, panthers and bears of Pa's stories might as well have been dodos or mastodons for all I hoped to see of one. Around here the greatest outdoor threat was irradiated corn. I did spot a basset hound, but when I pulled over, he ran away, balls flapping. Not a story for the grandchildren.

Grandma and Grandpa from the Books (Pa's parents) were originally from New England but moved to Illinois in 1842, and then to Wisconsin in 1850. The Quiners (Ma's parents) began east (New Haven, Connecticut), also to eventually settle in Wisconsin. I have heard people complain about lack of dating opportunities everywhere I've ever lived, but there really weren't a whole lot of options in rural Wisconsin in the 1860s. When all was said and done, three Quiners (Henry, Eliza, Caroline) married three Ingalls

(Polly, Peter, Charles). Charles and Caroline married in 1860. Peter Ingalls and Eliza Quiner Ingalls and Ma and Pa purchased eighty acres of land together in the woods of Pepin County. This property was my first destination.

January 10, 1865: Mary Amelia Ingalls was born, the same birthday as her father.

February 7, 1867: Laura Elizabeth Ingalls was born.

The little gray cabin sat off to the left of Little House Wayside, weathered and sturdy, resolutely performing its tourist duty. This replica had been built in 1977. A semicircle park had been carved from the surrounding cornfields, the stalks creating an agricultural stockade fence. Aside from the cabin, I saw a few trees, a little wandering room and some picnic tables.

I completed my outfit in the gravel drive. I wriggled in the crisscross apron straps, tied a bow in back, smoothed down the front and shook out my skirts. I fastened the bonnet under my neck but let it hang down my back so I could brown properly. All set, I checked out my reflection in the car window. I still didn't look nineteenth century so much, but at least I was less Wild West madam and more Nebraskan housewife trying to spice up her marriage. To me, the costume was complete.

For my first task, I cased the cornstalk perimeter. The grass was wet, and my feet slid around in my red flip-flops. I had grown up amidst the rolling green and humidity, and it was strange to visit this climate as a tourist, to be so aware of how wet air feels. Montana had been in the throes of forest fire season when I left, the entire Missoula valley so parched a few people had even broken out gas masks. The Wisconsin rain soothed my scratchy throat and plumped my cheeks. My skin felt dewy, as I realized it always had before, only I never thought about it. The dividing lines of my Alabama youth had always been North and South, but my thoughts shifted East and West.

A handicapped access ramp led up to the cabin. The door was unlocked, and I let myself in to a main room with a fireplace and two small rooms off to the side. The cabin was empty except for a few posters and a picnic table wedged in the corner. My nose caught the faint, musty whiff of absence; Ma wasn't there to mind the store. I ran from room to room trying to imagine what this would have been like furnished and with a family. I put my copy of *Big Woods* on the mantel, stepped back and admired my decorative touch. What if a log cabin had been my childhood home? It could be that if I had helped Mom churn butter instead of stuffing my face with hydrogenated snacks, I would be a different woman today. I had been a high-strung, fearful kid, conscious of how I annoyed people. If twenty kids leapt from the swing, I was the one who balked. I would eventually work up the nerve to launch, only to face-plant because I hesitated. I have memories of teachers and classmates irritated over my tears, telling me to buck up as I wailed over dead bugs. Probably I would meet myself at age six and not like me. It was only as Laura that I was self-possessed and brave.

I have an Olan Mills studio portrait of Laura and me, taken when I was a little girl. Family legend has it that I refused to leave the house unless Laura could come, too. Backdrop Number 8, Sandstone Wash, hangs behind us. My hands rest on a carpeted platform as I devoutly read *These Happy Golden Years*. Undoubtedly the photographer had set up this same shot many times before, only with leather-bound family Bibles. In the photo, I display the book cover, the scene of Laura and Almanzo holding hands under a cottonwood. I remember loving the lilac dress Laura is wearing, how I traced the trim and ruffles with my finger, thrilling over the tiny curls around her cheeks.

This portrait is one of many childhood photos taken over the years, picture after picture featuring monogrammed sweaters, split rail fences and simulated fall foliage. My job as progeny was to wear costumes and hold props to mark the passage of time. For Easter I donned Swiss polka dots and held up my basket. Halloween I yelled "trick or treat!" and displayed my jack-o'-lantern. Confirmation I wore a white dress and gripped my rosary. I patiently submitted to the documentation, perched on Santa's lap in a red velvet jumper with gritted teeth. My mother and I waged mighty battles over the outfits I wore in these photos, the fussy blouses I *hated*, the square dresses from Grandma I would wear *over my dead body*. This trend, in fact, only stopped a few years ago, when it dawned on me that I was middle-aged, and no longer obliged to pose in seasonal sweaters.

What makes this picture different is that I am posing with Laura, my symbol of choice. I imagine this small victory gave me strength in the face of childhood indignities, the book working as a shield from the ever-flashing bulbs of the adult paparazzi. In most childhood photos my round, pale features look confused or plastic, but here I have an expression of contentment. The smile is subtle but genuine. Eyes glazed and serene. Perhaps that's what was different about my costume today, I thought, as I used the camera timer to take pictures of myself in front of the cabin. Even if I was experiencing flashes of self-doubt and foolishness, the blue-flowered dress was an outfit of my choosing.

Outside the cabin, the grind of gravel under wheels snapped me out of my reverie. I was no longer alone. The Harley rider turned off the rumbly engine of his bike and parked. He was portly, dressed in black and red leather, and sported a thick moustache.

Harleyman: "Hey, would you take my picture?"

Me: "I'm Laura Ingalls Wilder!"

Harleyman: "How about here in front of the cabin?"

From Harleyman I learned that Highway 35 around Lake Pepin was a designated Harley scenic drive, which explained all the bikers I had seen. He didn't seem all that worried about a grown woman in a girl dress, or all that interested either. I discovered he was also from Alabama, but Dothan, and that he was retired and traveling around on his bike. We chatted for a while about how we had loved the Books as a kid, before he moseyed on so he could continue tracing our country's highways.

That afternoon most tourists took a quick photo from the car, barely slowing down in the circular drive. I don't know if they scurried away because of me, or if they slowed down to take a picture because of me, or if a drive-by was normal. Of those who bothered to actually park and get out, most would glance at me for a moment and walk away. For those who didn't run off, I offered the little historical spiel I had learned from the pamphlet, which they absorbed politely. They had probably just read it. Quite a few visitors asked me to take their picture, and some asked to have their picture taken with me, so I imagine I've shown up in some family slideshows. After a while I began to get in the swing of my role and relax a bit.

Out of all the people I talked to, only one woman asked me what I was doing.

"I'm just dying to know," she claimed.

"I'm on a quest," I said, stunned into the truth.

"Oh. A quest for what?"

I explained the green M&M's, a southern childhood, how I once built an entire frontier village out of Lincoln Logs, the emptiness of Big Wheeling in a cul-de-sac, *The Myth of Sisyphus* and the Jell-O mold of my soul that never took.

"I'd better get back to my niece and her friend," she said.

It was strange to loiter. We Americans tend to favor a "get 'er done" approach to sightseeing. Most people took about five to ten minutes to look around before they took off in search of a cheeseburger. I found myself growing restless as well, except I had just driven 1,259 miles to get here. I tried to reconnect my sense of purpose. Perhaps I should refine my talk. I could come out here every day and give renegade tours, eventually working myself into a permanent job. Then again, I might get arrested, or worse, become the subject of a film student's documentary. I was mulling over the possibilities on the picnic bench when I heard the gravel crunch one more time.

A minivan pulled up and parked. I was expecting a family or maybe a retired couple. Instead, one by one, a troop of Amish women emerged. It made sense that the Amish would be Laura fans.[1] They probably admired her moral imperative, family values and fascination with hand-hewn, wooden implements. I had never seen any Amish before that day, except those played by actors. The women's dresses were not movie plain, but truly plain; pastel, monochrome floral prints with unadorned hems. Their skin did

---

[1] Technical note: I didn't ask if these people were Amish or Mennonite so I'll never know for sure.

not have the fresh-faced glow of natural makeup, but the utter translucence of no makeup. I realized how much Caucasian eyes depend upon eyeliner to appear as though they exist.

Well—nothing says awkward like standing at a Laura Ingalls homesite dressed as a neon prairie tramp while an Amish book club piles out of a Dodge Caravan wearing calico and head garments for real. I became intensely aware of my tweezed eyebrows, Rouge Bingo lipstick and Wonderbra.

Feeling like a jerk wasn't my only problem. I had to pee. Peeing in costume in front of Amish women was out of the question. I don't mean to say there wasn't a facility, but I didn't want them to see me walking in there, knowing what goes on inside. It was wrong. In all nine books—through locusts, prairie fire and scarlet fever— no member of the Ingalls family ever pees. The family erects log cabins, shanties, haystacks, smokehouses and stables, but never an outhouse. Conceding defeat, I retreated to Room One of the Lake Pepin Inn, where I sat in the Amish rocker, cradling the remote in my palm, telling myself I could quit after just one episode.

In *Big Woods* Laura visits Pepin in a chapter called, with typical Laura brevity, "Going to Town." This was the first time she ever saw houses clumped together made of boards instead of logs. Lake Pepin was only a few blocks away from the inn, and I staved off Detectives Benson and Stabler by bribing myself with a visit to the waterfront. It was dusk as I walked down the quiet streets lined with refurbished historic buildings to the shore. The town was more wooded than the countryside, making the landscape more scenic, and perhaps closer in appearance to the nineteenth century. During Laura's time, Pepin was a rugged trading outpost. Steamboats traveled up and down the Mississippi hauling potatoes, lumber, furs, grain and other goods. Today, Pepin was a quaint tourist town of 878 residents, touted as a top day trip from the Twin Cities. Restaurants, pubs, shops and bed and breakfasts entertained upper-middle-class Midwesterners who came to sail their boats and sip Chardonnay. But while Pepin presented a certain buff and polish, it remained unpretentious. A visitor could dine on line-caught salmon wrapped in parchment, or shop for fish bait and suitcases of Bud Light at the gas station. The town logo was "Spend a day, a week, a lifetime," and you know, I checked out the prices of real estate.

Lake Pepin, a swell in the Mississippi, was larger than I expected, with blue-gray choppy waves. This expanse was Laura's first wide-open space so I imagine it was quite a wonder to her. Suspension bridges bookended the lake, and tree-lined escarpments rose from the water. Bluffs, parapets of layered limestone, sandstone and shale bedrock painted broad horizontal strips against the forest green. The sun lowered beyond the hills, turning the overcast sky shades of mauve and smoke, with a thin slice of seashell pink on the horizon. A few diehard water-skiers milked the last of the day, and a family posed for pictures on a bench. Further down Highway 35 was a town called Maiden Rock, named for a Dakota Indian woman, Wenona, who leapt off a cliff to escape the marriage arranged by her father, Chief Red Wing, who would go on to inspire a brand of sturdy shoes.

Out on the lake, the Pepin Yacht Club's piers hooked paths in the water. The boats were tucked in for the night, sails wrapped securely around the booms, halyards clanging on metal masts. I sneaked down to the private beach, but the polished, trucked-in sand was too civilized for my taste. I clambered farther down and traced the shoreline, navigating the rocks until I found a remote boulder to use as a perch. Unlike the razed forests, the lake looked to me like what Laura saw. I soaked up the peace that comes from a large body of water. Railroad tracks circled Lake Pepin, and I heard a train chugging in the distance, the sound growing louder. Laura wouldn't see her first train until she was a young teenager in Tracy, Minnesota, but I knew she would have loved watching the freight snake around the lake. The train made its way around and roared twenty feet behind me, beside me, and then past like those "In Stereo" recordings from the fifties.

The horn blast and clack of the wheels sparked a brief echo of the excitement I felt as a kid over skipping stones and chasing waves. I was able to coax the ghost emotion into a flutter before it flopped with a thud, pretty much like Luke Skywalker in his first attempts to master the force. Jedi Master Obi-Wan Kenobi called his disciple's weakness fear, and I suspected I suffered the same problem. I had avoided risk as an adult, scared to want things that would never happen, or that wouldn't be as great as I hoped, nervous I would launch and face-plant. I had anticipated too many bags of horehound candy only to find a stale bagel.

But the flutter was a start.

I swished my skirt. Now that I was relieved of performance duties, the costume was fun. I loved my fringe cowgirl shirt when I was six. I loved my Aimee Mann 'Til Tuesday hair in the eighties. I loved my rock and roll clothes from my twenties, which still live in a separate drawer. I suspect I stayed in bands so long just for a legitimate reason to buy and wear silver sparkle pants. On some level this Laura trip was another excuse to play dress up.

Gathering my orange ruffle so it wouldn't droop in the water, I fingered the pretty rocks in different colors: rose, granite gray, spotted black and white, tawny stripes. Like Laura, I was greedy and took too many. I crunched the gravel between my toes as the waves lapped my feet. The pink sky drifted below the trees. I took a stick and poked a fish skull, sat on my rock and listened to trains.

CHAPTER THREE
OF TRUTHS UNIVERSALLY ACKNOWLEDGED

Missoula, Montana: *Farmer Boy*

> *Three days shy of her fifteenth birthday, Alison Pope paused at the top of the stairs.*
>
> *Say the staircase was marble. Say she descended and all heads turned. Where was {special one}?*
> —George Saunders, "Victory Lap"

The Books have long been praised for their historical accuracy and fine moral character, but let's be honest, a big reason we keep coming back is the love story. The only competing literary romance, to my mind, is *Pride and Prejudice*. The flaw with *P & P*, though, is that Mr. Darcy and Elizabeth Bennett are works of fiction. In real life, Jane Austen was unlucky in love. Elizabeth Bennett might be the closest representation of the author we will ever know, and historians have speculated that Mr. Darcy was based on a real romance. Jane Austen deserved to meet an intelligent, good-looking (but not too good-looking), sensible man of independent means and integrity.

But no.

That is the best part about Laura and Almanzo: they were real and so was their lifelong love. Laura was able to write romantically about her husband after fifty years of marriage—a good sign. Almanzo is only nine at the time of *Farmer Boy*, but you can sense Laura's affection for him and his family. Later in the series, when Laura meets Almanzo as an adult, he might be "older, a homesteader," but the reader knows that he is simply a later model of the lovable kid who tortured himself over the ethics of a milk-fed pumpkin. Throughout the courtship Almanzo proves himself brave, skilled, reliable and romantic, a swain worthy of Laura's hand. Even better, long after the timeline of the Books, we know that Laura and Almanzo—her Manly—lived together into old age, having the marriage everyone dreams of, standing by one another until the end. When Laura rode off with Almanzo at the end of *These Happy Golden Years*, they went the distance.

Laura always did set the bar high.

My friend Anna said to me once, "Kelly, you have great taste in everything but men."

The memoir/tome *Kelly's Relationships and Where They Went Wrong* would make for lousy reading—no one would believe a woman could make such a series of poor decisions. When I was a young girl reading of Laura and Almanzo, I had no idea that my love life would be a series of flings, thangs, platonic gay boyfriends, platonic straight boyfriends, hookups, affairs, rebounds, erstwhile exes from Texas, resurrections and outright delusions. And I'm afraid this list makes my love life seem more interesting than it was. Mostly, I was single. I suspect it was these stretches of loneliness that made my otherwise exceptionally good taste falter.

Before I moved to Montana, the last boyfriend did me in with his emotional haranguing. Some days he ran hot, other times a twenty-minute drive too much of a sacrifice. Around the third time Mr. Fibby Ditherpants had "car trouble," I couldn't help but compare my lame suitor to Almanzo driving his horses twenty-four miles round-trip in the subzero Dakota winter—when a man wants to see you, distance isn't a problem. The effect on my historically low self-esteem had not been good.

"That guy was a tool," Anna said.

I vowed to remain alone until I met someone worth meeting. My resolve was admirable, but as months whipped by like calendar pages in an old movie, my concern grew.

Then I moved West, and the very first person I met was my poet cowboy.

It was after ten but still sunny in Montana when he introduced himself outside Al and Vic's, a local bar voted "stiffest drinks" by the *Missoulian*. Dressed in a black snap shirt, blue jeans and boots, his black hair swept in a wave over blue eyes.

Good-looking, I thought. *But not too good-looking.*

As we bonded over a few bourbons that proved the reviews correct, I began to consider that the Universe wasn't hateful, but on a tough-love plan. If I moved in a positive direction, then my stars aligned—just like the self-help books said.

From first cuddle, I knew we were meant for one another. He was warm. I am a reptile, and without sun, blood does not circulate through my body. During cold Montana nights, I clung to him like the skirt rail around a potbelly stove. My poet cowboy wasn't much for small talk, exuded a quiet but sturdy presence and enjoyed healthy portions at meals. It probably comes as no great shock that I began to call my new boyfriend Almanzo, or, My Manly.

The couple story is the best story, if you are in the couple. *How we met. That shirt you were wearing. The first kiss. The first time I realized that...* I stored each of these memories so that My Manly and I would have plenty to reflect upon in old age. I memorized the books he kept on his shelf, mentally recorded important dates, dried flowers and pressed them in a book. (Okay, technically, he only gave me one flower, but I kept it. On our first real date he bought me a rose from a flower lady. Not that I'm a rose person. Actually, I was kind of mortified, but upon reflection liked that he was nice to the flower lady.) My Manly was great at those kitschy yet delightful presents, and my apartment collected treasures, just as Laura's family did through their travels. A sparkly jewel flask. Scooby Doo press-on tattoos. A Japanese Maneki Neko welcome cat. For Valentine's I received a goopy, red velvet, heart-shaped box of candy that (once consumed) I used to collect restaurant matchbooks and notes we wrote one another on cocktail napkins.

We embarked upon a relationship based on fried chicken, fine whisky and *Buffy the Vampire Slayer*. We took roadside adventures around Montana. Helena. Anaconda. Whitefish. We went to the Sip 'n' Dip lounge in Great Falls, a tiki bar where women in mermaid costumes swim in a pool, and piano player Pat has played "Ring of Fire" five nights a week for the past thirty years. We met friends out for two-stepping and local brew. By *Buffy*, Season Five, our heroine ran to plunge herself into an alternate universe in yet another act of noble sacrifice, thus saving the world from apocalypse. (Again.) I sobbed hopelessly and burrowed my head into My Manly's shoulder.

This all felt suspiciously like happiness.

Then, as Buffy would say, the troubles came. My Manly began showing symptoms of Male Commitment Freak-Out Syndrome. He would disappear for a few days. He didn't "know." He didn't want to get us in a yo-yo pattern. He wasn't sure he knew what love was. He couldn't say what was wrong with him. "It" was all very complicated. Maybe he ate a poison doughnut. Or blame the waxing-waning moons in Jupiter. He broke things off—

—but then we would find ourselves sitting on my front stoop clutching one another's hands.

"I don't want to be here without you," I said one night. "You are my best Montana friend."

"You are my best friend anywhere," he said. The stricken look I was coming to know washed over his face. I wanted to reach for him but stopped myself. This had to be his idea.

My Manly had a basement apartment, and for the next few weeks I felt as though I were smoking out a badger. Patience might be a virtue, but it's not mine. More than once I almost threw my cell phone into the Clark Fork to keep myself from calling. I would stand on the Higgins Bridge, staring down at the churning water below. There's a man-made rapid called Brennan's Wave where kayakers practice their moves. I would watch them paddle and flip, paddle and flip, feeding off their dogged resolve. I clung to thoughts of Laura during *The Long Winter*. If she could subsist on coarse brown bread for seven months, I could wait one more day. A smarter woman would have taken the hint, but faith operates on the principle of belief, not probabilities. I had decided to believe.

I'd reached a bizarre, trancelike state when the email arrived. I stared stupidly for a solid minute before I clicked the message open. There it was. Everything I had been waiting to hear since I was three days shy of my fifteenth birthday. My Manly was tired of observing life and was ready to live it. With me. What he loved about me: my loyalty to my friends, how I bought the good chicken,

31

that I put my finger in his pocket and said "finger in yer pocket!" Best of all, he loved that I wanted to traipse around the Midwest dressed as Laura Ingalls Wilder. Yes, he was a no-talk-aholic, but he wanted to be different. I made him want to be different.

Such was my new Western life. Miracles happened. We made up right before my trip. Before I left, My Manly gave me a tiny stuffed, shiny sea turtle made of satin. The creature was chartreuse and aqua blue, with little black beads for eyes, and wee flipper feet. He was stuffed with something pebbly so he had a bit of heft.

"A mascot," he said.

I took Mr. Turtle and placed him on my palm. Now I understood. My Manly wasn't an ornery badger, but a turtle; reserved and pokey to the point of frustration, but not mean. I petted Mr. Turtle's shiny green head with my finger and placed him on the center of my Camry dash, where he gave the gray plastic a bright cheery feel. My Manly and I hugged and kissed good-bye. As usual he didn't say much, but that was fine. Talking about the relationship wasn't my strong suit either. Our future remained vague, and I was still shaky from the past few weeks, but Mr. Turtle would be the difference between traveling alone and traveling lonely.

CHAPTER FOUR
BOUNDARY ISSUES

Independence, Kansas: *Little House on the Prairie*

That is happiness; to be dissolved into something complete and great.
—Willa Cather, *My Antonia*

Three hundred forty-two miles into Kansas I encountered another Sign: *Verdigris River.*

I pulled over to inspect the small but sturdy brown river that led Pa, Ma, Mary, Laura and Baby Carrie to their Kansas claim 120 years ago, but I didn't linger. I wanted to make the homesite with plenty of daylight to spare, and even after all my driving, I had more driving to go.

When first planning my trip, I worried how all this solitary travel was going to sit with me. Most road trippers blast through the Plains gripping a bucket of coffee. Nobody targets the Corn Belt to grid surf. Compounding the matter was my decision to travel two-lane highways, as I wanted to see Prairieland, not Interstateville. Although more scenic, these roads meant my long, remote drives would be even longer and more remote. I had to slow to 35 mph for every post office. I got stuck behind combines. I slept alone in far-flung motor courts. My cell phone cut out. I could very easily have cracked or turned inside out from boredom as I cruised an endless vista of corn, soybeans and fescue.

I discovered I loved it.

Traveling alone holds a certain kind of magic. Reading is a solitary act, and my relationship with Laura had always been one-on-one.

Solo turned out to be the perfect way to fly. I didn't have to deal with snarky rejoinders that might break the spell. I didn't have to deal with intelligent or sincere comments, for that matter. I was free to live in my own thoughts, musings, fantasies, marvels, or I could zone out and think nothing at all. The Books rode shotgun, and Mr. Turtle flopped on the dash. I kept a bag of Cheetos handy so I could paw through that crunchy, cheesy, FD&C Orange No. 5 goodness. I guzzled Coke and belched freely. I couldn't have been more complete if Jack the faithful bulldog were trotting under the Camry.

Prairie people such as myself, I discovered, find a vast landscape relaxing. Travel became a form of stasis, a suspension from linear time. The more I drove, the more big sky filled my child of grunge, "Black Hole Sun" heart. When I first heard Kurt Cobain unleash his guttural scream of suburban misery I thought, *Yes, that's exactly right.* As the odometer spun, I smelled less like teen spirit and more of fresh-cut hay and cornflowers. To experience Laura's landscape in 3-D created a delicious sense of unreality. I was high on prairie Prozac.

In *Little House*, Laura describes Kansas as a vast expanse of flat land covered in tall grasses blowing in the wind. She and her family travel for days and see nothing but this endless land and rippling grass, all capped by a "perfect circle" of sky curving down to the land, with their wagon in the center of that circle. Laura's grasses had long been plowed into a farmscape, but the circle remained. My two-lane highway, then, became a diameter bisecting the circle, my Camry forever a point of geometry in space. Trees jutted out here and again along with flagpoles flying crisp Old Glories. A gentle puffiness to the clouds hinted of southern sky, but the air felt western, too. Kansas was neither here nor there, yet utterly present. This circle of prairie was the portal between worlds. No wonder L. Frank Baum chose Kansas as the gateway to Oz.

If you have never stood in the middle of a prairie, try it. Wear a dress that rustles. Take in the wide-angle lens of soft, blue sky. You can see for miles. Hawks! Wind rushing through grass sounds like the ocean, only more relaxing, for while the swish-sound might surge and wane, it never crashes. When a gust gathers special intensity, you feel an ion charge, a silver tingle that shoots up your spine. Then a bug flies up your nose and you bolt for the car.

The Kansas homesite blended seamlessly with the prairie. I only knew to stop because I saw a section of split rail wood fence—that, and a little log cabin.

A chief advantage to the Prairieland vacation over theme parks was plenty of parking close to attractions and no crowds. On the downside, I was sometimes the only visitor, a little weird. Once more, I had to mentally bolster myself before I could emerge from the car in this dress. Once more, I found the best way to do something was to do it. I couldn't say that I had conquered all my childish fears, but with each stop I found myself hesitating less and less. A fiftyish woman sat hunched behind the gift shop cash register. She wore a gray tunic and a facial expression much like Jack the faithful bulldog. A buzzing fly dive-bombed and fell dead on the windowsill.

"Hi," I croaked, my voice out of practice.

"Hello," she said. Her eyes flickered briefly alive before glazing back over.

My first instinct was retreat, but after all the driving, rushing back out seemed silly. Was I not supposed to linger, enjoy this moment? *Don't get weird*, I told myself. *Chill out and shop.* I glanced over at the cashier again. Nothing. I thought about asking where something was to jump-start conversation, but I could see everything. The gift shop was one room. A quick scan informed that the shop carried many of the same items as in Pepin, only printed with the particular site name. Charlotte rag dolls. Metal lunch pails. School slates and chalk.

Laura's stories transition smoothly into souvenir shopping, as every book is well-supplied with attachment objects. *Little House* features the tin cup, the sparkly heart cake and the shiny Christmas penny from Mr. Edwards, while mainstays such as Pa's fiddle span the entire series. When reading the Books, I track the appearance of every item in a mental spreadsheet. These family talismans have always been a source of great comfort. Every talisman, that is, except for the one that has always been a source of great anxiety. When I passed a little shelf of replica China shepherdesses, I experienced a familiar constriction of the throat.

Every time I read the Books, I am convinced the fragile doll will not survive the journey intact, or that Laura will spaz out and smash her. Disaster is part of every book, but so long as the shepherdess endures, we know everything will be okay. Only Ma can be trusted with the sacred symbol, and I cannot relax until Ma has placed the doll in the center of the mantel in each home.

Once a friend gave me a present of Spiegelau wineglasses. Eighteen white. Eighteen red. Today, of the original thirty-six, five remain. Make that four. If I were a superhero, my name would be Shatterglass. My mother has a collection of fine porcelain (more than two hundred pieces total). She has never chipped a tea cup. When I visit my parents I ensconce myself in bubble wrap and try not to move. Flutterbudgets such as Laura and I are best kept far away from the collectibles.

Only Ma's handle the china.

I tiptoed past the brittle shepherdesses on to more durable souvenirs. I lean toward coffee mugs and refrigerator magnets, which I still chip, but the bummer is manageable. My plan was to collect the covered wagon refrigerator magnet from each homesite. That way I could build a wagon train to surround my Maine lobster amputee and terra cotta Alamo with the cracked bell tower.

I made another attempt to engage the cashier, pulling back my lips in an attempted *See? I'm normal* smile. Not a twitch. Not a blink. I wondered if the woman had completed Beefeater training and this job was her final test. I don't know what I expected from a person sentenced to work a cash register all day in rural Kansas.

Perhaps:

"Hello, Laura! What a pretty dress! I can tell just by looking that you have a deep spiritual connection to our heroine that surpasses the average tourist. Might I offer you a frosty lemonade?"

I could tell I was perking up a bit because I worked a little butter churn (as in the dance move) by the postcard tree.

Quick—I slunk my eyes askance.

Nothing.

These meth heads are everywhere now, I imagined her thinking. *I can't wait to get home and eat my slow cooker pork roast. Meat should be falling off the bone about now.*

For My Manly I selected a coffee mug with a Monet-esque Laura running across a prairie, so he could think of me as free and pastoral with his morning brew. For my friend Anna I bought the mug with a rustic glaze as to invoke the simple joys of country livin'. I rounded out my purchases with a bookmark plus the donation/ticket to the homesite.

"Thanks," I whispered, while Ms. Beefeater duly placed my purchases in a bag.

There was, as we recall, a problem with the Ingalls family's decision to settle Kansas in 1869. People already lived there. The family staked their claim in the Osage Diminished Reserve, home to seven bands of the Osage Nation. Pa didn't realize his error because he didn't register his claim. He was, and there is no way to say this gently, a squatter. Pa crossed a line.

Initially, settlers had no interest in this land, as early nineteenth-century surveyors had proclaimed the Great Plains an uninhabitable wasteland. In 1806, the American explorer, Zebulon Pike, took a route through the Sandhills region, which he compared to the African desert. A second expedition in 1820 concurred with Pike's assessment. For years, huge cursive letters pronounced "Great American Desert" across the center of North American maps and globes.

The Great Plains remained ignored by the United States government until 1830, when President Andrew Jackson decided to claim the South for white settlement and passed the Indian Removal Act. The idea was that tribes could trade their lands east of the Mississippi for lands west. Conveniently enough, the Great American Desert was available. The trades were considered voluntary, but in truth had all the freedom of *Sophie's Choice*— respecting boundaries wasn't Old Hickory's strong suit. The most infamous consequence was the Trail of Tears, in which four thousand Cherokee died in a brutal forced march. By 1837, the

Jackson administration had removed forty-six thousand Native American people, and white settlers gained access to twenty-five million acres.

Later, the American government realized their mistake. Not the Trail of Tears part, but not recognizing Kansas as desirable farmland. Washington again plotted to (re)relocate the Indians. In 1854, Congress passed the Kansas-Nebraska Act, opening the country to settlement. This act, in turn, embroiled the area in the nation's great slave debate as Northern abolitionists and Southern slaveholders raced to claim territory. Ultimately, the abolitionists won and Kansas was admitted as a free state in 1861. The Kansas government (for a brief while) even recruited blacks to their state. Laurafans will recall that the Ingalls family, when they contracted malaria, had a black doctor. (Dr. Tan's grave resides in Independence. Laura spelled his name in *Little House* Dr. Tann.)

When the Ingalls family encountered the Osage, the tribe had already relocated once, due to a treaty signed in 1808. They ceded homeland on the Osage River and moved to western Missouri, followed by a push farther west to Kansas. Originally, the Osage had only traveled to Kansas for buffalo hunting trips. This relocation might not have been so bad, except white settlers had already sacked the hunting grounds. In the early 1800s, thirty million buffalo covered the Great Plains. By 1850 this number was down to twenty million. In 1870, the same year the Ingalls family lived in Kansas, the animal went extinct. That's why Laura describes gophers, jackrabbits, prairie chickens, blackbirds and wolves in her prairie travels, but never a buffalo.

In *Little House*, Pa's building of the log cabin is described in exacting detail. The erection of the frame. The laying of the puncheon floor. The construction of the hearth, rock by rock. Whoever built the replica cabin appeared to have followed Pa's lead; it had good thick walls that could keep little girls safe from wolves. The logs were rough hewn, and the flaws gave the cabin a nice authentic feel. I could imagine Pet and Patty the western mustangs hauling these trees from Walnut Creek.

The interior differed slightly from the book's illustration. The red-checkered tablecloth was in position, but the metal glider looked out of place. Also, Garth Williams had the furniture arranged differently, and he ran the puncheon floor up and down versus left to right. Williams was probably inaccurate on this count—logs that long would have been scarce on the prairie. I suspect he drew the planks to create perspective and make the room appear larger. These discrepancies didn't worry me too much, as my only real beef was with the replica shepherdess. She was off to the left, and everybody knows the shepherdess belongs dead center. Some jerk must have moved her—some jerk who forgot *only Ma touches the shepherdess.*

I stood in the doorway, in all my five-foot-nine, milk-fed glory. Laura employs adjectives such as cozy and snug when describing her houses, but little is perhaps the most accurate. People were a great deal shorter then, which undoubtedly helped. Laura's nickname of Half-Pint was no exaggeration; she never cleared five feet as an adult. My family is tall. I've caught our group reflection in retail windows and can't help but notice how we resemble giraffes gliding across the Serengeti.

I eyeballed the cabin. It would have been tight, but the Fergusons (Dad, Mom, Kelly, younger brother Tim) could have fit. At first, the thought of growing up with my family in one room struck me as a nightmare. Had I not spent enough time in therapy already? Then I reconsidered. I thought back to when we took family camping trips in an orange Volkswagen bus. I would sleep in the pop-up hatch, while my brother slept in a cot that stretched over the front seats. Mom and Dad took the foldout bed. I remember feeling comforted to know my parents were right below me, even if their breath was sour. I was safe.

In our suburban house, I had my own room with a double bed. My parents told me how lucky I was, but I often woke up in the middle of the night, anxious. Some nights I slept balled up, terrified of the space. I wanted to sleep in my parents' room, a warm, comforting place from which I was generally ejected. In the pioneer days, parents couldn't kick the kids out. When you had a bad dream Ma and Pa were right there. If I had grown up in this small cabin, I would have spent every day surrounded by provisions, my protectors close by. It occurred to me that while the slogan of my youth was "I'm bored," maybe what I meant was "I'm lonely."

The Ingalls family lived in close quarters, but then they were isolated from their neighbors, as were most pioneers. The big square claims were staked in a way that put great distances between everyone. I had always been haunted by the story of the two bachelors in *Little House* who built one log cabin on their shared property line so they wouldn't have to live alone. In the twenty-first century, Americans continue the isolation trend by living in suburbs and gated communities. Supposedly, these boundaries are so we can feel safe, but if so, then why all the modern anxiety? It could be we don't need antidepressants so much as company.

Regarding Indian/settler relations, many current versions of history confirm Laura's stories. Language barriers made communication difficult. The cultures had different expectations in everything from clothing to home construction. The settlers feared the Indians and considered homesteading their imperative to "civilize" the land. The Indians, in turn, suffered relocations, genocide and devastation of their lands. Sometimes they retaliated—violently. The "jamboree" that takes place toward the end of *Little House* was a documented event, as the Osage debated whether they should move peacefully or fight.

In therapy, one of the first skills taught is that of recognizing boundaries, learning how to separate your emotions from those of others, especially those of your family. I suspect that for the Osage, emotional boundaries might have been a moot topic, not just within the family, but within the larger group. Home wasn't so much a square section of land, or the dwelling, but the people living and traveling as a unit. Laura relates a story of Indians coming in the house and taking Pa's tobacco and asking Ma to cook some cornbread. Many Kansas pioneers have related similar stories. The Osage thought nothing of helping themselves to whatever food they wanted, causing me to wonder if I may, in fact, be part Osage. The first thing I do at someone's house is open the fridge.

Laura's fixation on wanting to see a "papoose" has been criticized in these more socially aware times. Granted, her comparison of a "papoose" to baby deer and rabbits that Pa has shown her is less than politically correct. (I should also clarify that the very word papoose is listed in my dictionary as a term that is "dated and offensive.") In Laura's defense ("Laura" here meaning both the little girl and the author trying to remember what it was like to be a little girl), I imagine that an Osage infant would have seemed quite glamorous to a Victorian child who, as they say, didn't get out much. Difference fascinates. Kids, I've noticed, don't think of different as bad, just terribly interesting. When I was a girl, I had an Indian mother doll that held a swaddled brown infant with black glossy eyes. The papoose (as in the carrier) was glued on, but I kept picking at the fabric. I had to know what that Indian baby underneath looked like. What if it was different from my white baby dolls? After hours of labor, I discovered the Indian baby had the same flat plastic front, only browner.

Indians were likewise fascinated with white babies. One nineteenth-century Kansas mother wrote in her journal the story of two Indian mothers who rode up while she was berrying. They stopped when they saw the baby. One Indian mother held out her arms, and the infant (to the shock of the mother) went right to her. The Indian women passed the pioneer woman's eight-month-old baby around, laughing and exclaiming, "Oh, petite papoose!" while the mother (who feared Indians) quietly freaked out to the side.

My point: all cultures objectify babies, yet no one ever stops to consider how they hold up under the constant expectation of adorableness.

I was quickly figuring out that while the replica cabins were fine and all, it was prairies and waters that were my direct line to Laura. In *Little House*, Walnut Creek was where minnows nibbled Laura's feet and she picked all the blackberries she wanted. I had long venerated memories of Pa going down to cut trees for lumber and coming back again. Why this detail was so comforting I couldn't say, except I loved the idea of Pa coming and going.

My problem was that I had no idea where to look for the creek. The smart thing to do would have been to ask the gift shop clerk.

41

Instead, I walked down a road behind the cabin for no reason beyond an assumption that the creek would be "out back," and therefore a better direction to locate what Laura describes as "the bottoms." The road ended at a thin windbreak of trees. After a brief exploration in the woods, I found some water sludge that looked like a breeding ground for mosquitoes. Still water such as this caused the "fever 'n' ague" (malaria) that beset the Ingalls family—a promising start— but I expected more. Barbed wire marked off private land to my right, with a defunct pumpjack jutting out the middle like a grazing steel horse. The forbidden land taunted me. It was possible that sludge was all that remained, but I fretted that the real Walnut Creek with running water was beyond the fence. The creek with long-legged water bugs skating over glassy-still pools, where green-coated frogs with white chests plopped in the water, and wood pigeons called among the trees and the brown thrush sang. I stopped and gave pause. Like Laura, I struggled with my conscience and the part of me that is naughty inside. Trespassing was wrong. Illegal. Bad girl stuff.

But.

The creek.

I gave a quick scan of the horizon and clambered over the gate, maneuvering my dress and legs so they didn't catch. I landed in the pasture with a thud and took visual inventory. A quick survey confirmed that I was undetected, at least not by any people.

There might be a natural wonderland down by those trees, a veritable prairie Eden teeming with rabbits, tiny fish and dickybirds. A gurgling aquatic paradise. A Midwestern botanical display of verdant magnificence. I'll never know, because twenty steps into the pasture I was charged by a herd of black cattle beelining toward me in a mooing avalanche.

When people acquire a watch animal to guard the property, they usually get a dog, perhaps a bulldog like Jack, or a pair of Dobermans named Cossack and Ms. Khan. I suggest cows. I had always envisioned cows as docile creatures, stationary and chewing, jaws and flicking tails the only parts in motion. Cows move faster than you might think. I knew the cows weren't trying to attack me, they simply saw that I was human and therefore a supplier of food. But even if the cows weren't malicious in intent, that didn't mean I trusted them to brake properly.

I picked up my skirts and ran.

Bunching up my dress and apron, I scrambled back over the fence, scraping my leg as I swung back over and planted two feet soundly in front of the NO TRESPASSING sign. The agitated cows lowed and paced the fence, demanding grub. By Divine Providence, my skirt had not been torn or muddied. I exhaled in relief, thinking I had escaped retribution—when I turned around and saw the blue minivan.

I tried to think how I was going to play this. I hoped it wasn't the landowner, which would be an awkward encounter at best, and a nasty one at worst. Hiding was not a possibility. My bright blue dress made blending into the open prairie difficult. There was nowhere to go, no accomplice to blame, and a herd of accusatory cows mooing at me. Another realization: cows are loud. The window lowered, and a fiftyish Amish man with the telltale circle beard stuck his head out.

"Hi, Laura. Looking for the creek?"

The man's wife waved from the passenger's side. Looked like I wasn't the only vigilante Laurafan in town; the couple was here to scout out Walnut Creek as well. The man didn't seem at all shocked or disapproving of my behavior, only interested in what I had seen.

"Ah, you are Laura, I can tell. Always getting into scrapes."

We compared site visits, who had been where and such, but his primary interest was the door, the one Pa built with wooden pegs instead of nails. That's how plain Pa lived his life. He didn't even need nails. The man said he had spent hours poring over that passage both as a boy and an adult, and that someday his goal was to fashion a door just like that, which I said struck me as a fine ambition. The Amish couple parked so they could go check out the sludge and mosquitoes, even if that was all. We Laura sticklers are like that.

On the way back to my car, I took a closer look at the log cabin door, which truthfully I had not even noticed before. Interesting to me was how the Amish man and I extracted different meanings from the story. I had read that chapter many, many times but couldn't report much about how to build a door with wooden pegs. What

43

mattered to me was the emotional connection, that Laura was helping her Pa. Prairie Laura is a huge transition from Big Woods Laura. Laura has stepped through the magic circle; she's a big girl. With Baby Carrie part of the family, Laura is no longer the youngest. She takes on more responsibility and becomes Pa's stalwart helper.

I, too, was feeling stronger, getting my prairie legs. I tested them a little, jumping up and down in the grass.

After all the travel and the building and the plowing and the door constructing, the Ingalls family would live in Kansas for only one year. In *Little House* Pa claims that he refuses to dicker with the "men in Washington" over land rights with the Osage. He would rather leave. Hindsight reveals that Pa could have stayed. Predictably, Indians lost the land dispute.

There is, of course, no defense of the Indian genocide, and Charles Ingalls was one of many settlers who participated in the land takeover. But I do offer this final justification of Laura in *Little House*. The traditional line is that it's Ma who hates the Indians and Pa who is more sympathetic, while modern perspectives reveal both viewpoints as hegemonic. It's Laura, though (and therefore the author Laura as well), who through the voice of a child speaks the truth. When Ma complains about Indians, Laura asks what the family came here for, if they don't like them. Laura even contradicts the sacred Pa when he says that white people are going to settle this country, asking, but isn't this *Indian* territory? And won't asking them to leave make them *mad*? Both times she is shushed in the way parents do when asked difficult questions that require true and unsavory answers.

One of the last events in *Little House* is the scene where the Osage march out, creating a melancholy procession in front of the Ingalls cabin. Laura finally sees her Indian baby, but discovers that she should have been careful what she asked for—the child's eyes trouble her and then she can't stop crying.

It was time for me to move on as well. I said my good-byes to the cabin, to the Kansas prairie, to the Angus guard detail and even to the Beefeater.

On my way out, I found a roadside BBQ joint. What distinguishes Kansas BBQ from other varieties is that no animal escapes the smoker—beef brisket, ribs, turkey, pulled pork, pulled chicken, ham, hot links. I grabbed a big plate of carne and ate the tender, savory, flavory meat until I could eat no more. It was early evening, and the stars appeared hazy due to city lights and pollution, but they were trying to sparkle and get closer to me, I could tell.

Chapter Five
Rivals

Walnut Grove, Minnesota: *On the Banks of Plum Creek*

> *The art of war is of vital importance to the State. It is a matter of life and death, a road either to safety or to ruin. Hence it is a subject of inquiry which can on no account be neglected.*
> —Sun Tzu, *The Art of War*

In *Plum Creek*, Laura confronts the outside world and learns unpleasant truths. She survives her first heartbreak when Pa trades Pet and Patty, the Western mustangs, for oxen. She stands down a herd of runaway cows, an act of bravery I had recently come to appreciate. She has her first day of school. Her family experiences the first real threat to their pioneer dream when locusts devour their wheat crop. The toughest lesson of all, though, might be that people aren't always good and kind, that sometimes they are selfish, spiteful or just plain nasty. In *Plum Creek*, Laura meets archnemesis Nellie Oleson.

Kansas had taught me that I could enjoy traveling alone. My next step was to bring the outside world back into the mix, with all its complications. The closer I got to Walnut Grove, I began to agitate, thoughts of Nellie dredging up old resentments. My sense of justice has always been very keen. When wronged I can stew for months, sometimes years after the actual event. In many ways, this entire trip was an exercise in picking at childhood scabs, and as I approached the former Laura/Nellie battleground, I found myself reliving injustices from my past. I needed angry music as I confronted my destiny with evil, so I scream-sung Hole into the windshield. Courtney Love was the natural musical selection—like Nellie, she's blonde, rude and wears baby doll dresses.

Loving to hate Courtney Love is one of my favorite pastimes. No, Courtney Love hasn't ever abused me personally, as that would involve meeting her. But she has gotten everything I ever wanted by being awful—not fair. I was in love with Kurt Cobain, and we were to be married, until she got in the way. She had his baby. My band never made it past Greensboro, while Hole toured the world. Post-grunge, I endured Courtney's acting career, her fashion awards and the affair with Edward Norton, my other future husband. Justice hadn't been this skewed since the eighties, when Jessica Lange slept with Mikhail Baryshnikov and Sam Shepard in the same lifetime.

I can admit that part of my Courtney hate stems from jealousy. If she were a no-talent nobody, hating wouldn't be worth the effort. As much as a person might talk smack about her rival, she can't be weak, or there's no point. That's why Nellie Oleson was a worthy opponent. She had amazing toys and wouldn't share. She was blonde and pretty and charismatic, and her family owned a store filled with candy. She had everything, yet made the active choice to be horrid. That's why it's so satisfying when Laura takes her down.

My Courtney ritual begins when I put on some grunge that takes me back to the greasy-haired flannel years of my twenties. I ruminate on all the ways Courtney Love has ruined my life, ruined Kurt's life and ruined all of rock and roll, eventually working up to a backstage brawl scene. I read once that Courtney would get drunk and attack people in bars, as in physically, and that's when I knew—it was on.

Maybe Madonna took the high road when Courtney hurled a lipstick, but not me. I grab a Gibson SG and return fire, a chunky flash of silver and cherry wood lurching in the air, hovering for a second before it crashes on the ground. Roadies flee in terror. Courtney snarls and lunges. My right fist grabs the front of her smutty baby doll dress, and I pull as my left hook meets her jaw. She's not expecting a southpaw, and I make full contact. Crack!

The mile markers whizzed by as I embroiled myself in a typical Courtney-Kelly scenario. Anger is a great way to pass the time. I was all energy and boiling blood, wheels rolling beneath me as I passed field after field. I was gonna conquer this bitch. (The road? Courtney?)

Then I crossed the Minnesota state line.

Whooooooooooooooooooooooooooooaaaaaaaaaaaaaaaaaaaaaahhhhh.

The speed limit slowed from 65 to 55. Hello, Lutheran country, land of caution and black coffee. I immediately felt guilty for thinking the *B* word. Resigned, I set the cruise control, but slowing down made me sullen. I wanted to explain to Minnesota that Highway 14 was the same in other states, and there we had cruised quite safely at 65. But I had learned in South Dakota that conversations with state troopers tend to be one-sided. I needed to settle out and enjoy Niceland. Problem being, I didn't feel nice right now.

Lutheran country was new to me. Lutheranism isn't big in the South, as southerners prefer more drama in their religion, the way they require more seasoning in their food. Southerners might be conservative in that they are mostly pro-gun and pro-life, but the speed limit? That's flexible, y'all. In Montana, a person had to speed to avoid visibly aging between urban centers.

The situation called for a mental reset. I pulled over for a Dairy Queen banana crème pie Blizzard to soothe my throat—scream-singing is rough on the tonsils. I spooned creamy goodness and simmered down. Back in the car I adjusted to the slower pace and eased into a rural Minnesotan state of mind. Before long, I found myself craving tuna noodle casserole—light on the black pepper.

My brow was damp, and I turned up the AC. Lake Pepin and the cool forests of Wisconsin were far behind. I discovered that the Minnesota summer climate was humidsunnyhot, as in Alabama-level humidsunnyhot. My understanding had always been people moved north for cooler summers, but this was a heat that fuzzed the eyeballs. I drifted back into my slower southern ways. Soon, beating Courtney Love to a pulp began to strike me as unladylike and insensible, not to mention taxing.

I drove in silence, absorbing the hum of the car engine. The prairie lightened into a paler shade of verdant, and the hills ironed out. I became Farmer Moses parting a green sea of agriculture, fields and fields of corn punctuated by the occasional soybean crop, the agrarian variation of duck, duck, goose. The cruise control kept me honest, but the animals didn't follow state highway regulations. Gophers jaywalked. Pheasants ran stoplights. Swallows dive-bombed the car only to swoop away like bats. Often our furry friends didn't make it. I could only identify the skunks, whose corpses retained a lingering presence. I thought back to third grade when I could name every species of fuzzy mammal in North America, but my Golden Guide book never showed me what a raccoon looked like on the inside. Long after the buffalo's extinction, we Americans still cross the landscape to suit our own purposes, our destinations more important than ecology.

"It's not real," I told Mr. Turtle as we passed what appeared to have once been a member of his species.

Every fifteen miles or so, the highway spliced a blink-of-an-eye downtown. Gas station with a white cinder block store. Local café. Silo. Carryout liquor. Church. Tiny park with concrete benches like cuttlefish. I wouldn't have even believed such small towns existed anymore except I'd just driven through a hundred of them. The town of Revere requested I slow from 55 to 50 as I passed their gas station. Revere didn't ask much. Just a tip of the hat—howdy.

And a few miles later, but no hurry, no hurry now at all, another Sign: *Plum Creek.*

I was traveling 35 mph slower than when I witnessed the South Dakota Sign, so the braking went easier this time—no skid marks. I pulled over like a grandpa in his Coupe de Ville. When I swung the car door open, the sun assaulted and the whir of insects filled my ears. Within seconds the dress stuck to my skin. The glare was so fierce I could barely pry my eyes open, even when I cupped my hand as a shield. I desired nothing but retreat to the comfort of my air-conditioned car but forced my wussy modern self to remain outside for at least a few minutes. Under the bridge, a tiny brown ribbon worked its way through the Minnesota farmland. Eventually, that trail of water connected with Laura's old homestead.

The vertical, '70s neon sign of the Wilder Inn advertised the accommodations as modern, new and very nice. The neat U of rooms was a few yards off Highway 14. In Praireland, a traveler doesn't exit so much as stop. I had timed my trip to coincide with Walnut Grove's annual pageant, *Fragments of a Dream*, a production of *Plum Creek* put on for three weekends every summer. The influx of visitors to small-town America was apparent; a tour bus rumbled out front of the humble roadside motel.

The twenty-something groundskeeper checked me in. He was quick, wiry and tan, wearing an unbuttoned shirt, khaki shorts and work boots. A blonde planchette of chest hair matched the fuzz on his upper lip. He seemed in no hurry to walk away, and my bright blue dress flagged me as a tourist, so we chatted awhile, me fighting the urge to retreat to my room, take off this dress and read. I learned that a descendant of the actual Wilder family had stayed here recently, and I talked a little about my trip. He nodded that lots of people came here because of those Laura Ingalls books and asked if I was here for the pageant. I was. We discussed local food options, which didn't take long. I conveyed my desire for a nice salad and explained that, for me, a salad bound by mayo didn't count. A wedding reception was taking place across the street, and we idly watched the procession of polished cotton.

"Around here, people don't eat much salad. There's some corn-fed girls around here, if you know what I'm saying."

Something about how he said this made me believe he didn't think I looked corn-fed in my Laura dress. Wait. Was this the part in my quest where Kelly Got Her Groove Back? From the car Mr. Turtle cast a disapproving eye.

"Uh, my boyfriend lived in Iowa for a while," I said.

I admit my reply was a lame conversational segue based on a weak corn connection. It was a very transparent way of slipping in "my boyfriend." As I heard the words out loud, I realized I liked the idea that I belonged to somebody, and that somebody belonged to me. My boyfriend.

"He lived in a small town, and I believe there was lots of corn there," I struggled on.

"It's a small town around here all right."

"Well, everybody's gotta be from somewhere."

"Yeah, I guess I'll die here," he said, stuffing his hands in his pockets and looking down. He didn't seem too enthused over the prospect.

Conversations about death tend to kill a flirtation. The

groundskeeper shuffled off, gave me a feeble wave and told me to just let him know if I needed anything.

The next morning I gave the dress a good shake and suited up. This was how Laura lived, wearing the same outfit every day, and there was a certain comfort to the routine. My zipping and unzipping skills had improved. I knew to plan ahead where the metal teeth stuck in the middle, developing a nifty tuck and zoom move. The only problem was that I found myself dressed and on the road too fast. The quick drive to town likewise jarred me, as I had grown accustomed to long, pensive drives. The five-minute jaunt down Highway 14 didn't give me time to mentally prepare. Whenever Laura went to town, she had a nice, relaxing walk during which she could collect her thoughts. Before I knew it, another Sign was upon me: *Walnut Grove, Population 599.* I took in a quick cruise of the grid, which consisted of streets one through nine. In Laura's time, the head count came to 154, so the town hadn't grown much. The area's latest immigrant influx is the Hmong, who now account for about a quarter of the town's population, which explained the Asian grocery store I had passed earlier in nearby Tracy.

A quick turn off Main Street put me at Laura Central. The Plum Creek homesite was in the country, but as usual there were Laura sights to see and do in town. Pageant day had Laura Central at peak flow. A long row of minivans lined the dirt parking lot, and Midwestern families tumbled out. Girls in calico dresses and bonnets and boys in suspenders swung on the split rail fences. Ma's and Pa's tried to keep the crew organized the best they could as the frontier flea circus boinged around.

We all herded straight for the gift shop.

The prickly energy of consumption surrounded the building. Compared to the sparse attendance of the other homesites, this was a mob scene. The only other adults in frontier garb were the employees, except they wore neck-high, plain, Victorian dresses distinctly free of ribbons, puffed sleeves and traffic cone flounces. Everyone was mad for Laura booty. Magnets, bookmarks, spoons, figurines, aprons, tin cups, toys, candy, afghans, charm bracelets, prairie schooner toothpick holders, china bells, snow globes, pewter thimbles and ornaments. This was my biggest Laura gift shop to date, and I hadn't been part of a shopping frenzy either. I got a little caught up as I snagged an "I ♥ Laura" pin, a prairie dress and bonnet for Barbie and a cookie cutter in the shape of Pa's fiddle. Kids eyed my goods with envy. *Get your own Visa card*, I thought, and then I had to admit I was getting out of control. Reluctantly, I put back a Jack the Faithful Bulldog paperweight.

I was not prepared for what I saw next, although in retrospect I should have been. To believe I could escape this rival showdown had been naive on my part, a denial of the facts, a delusion. For there, on a shelf, sat an item that created a lurching pit at the very bottom of my gut, like a dead puppy in a gully.

A *Little House on the Prairie* '70s metal lunch box.

TV Laura and Mary's chipped paint faces stared me down, their plastered-on smiles daring me to challenge them.

There was no escaping this any longer.

Fluff your pillows, grab a snack and get comfy. The time has come to address a matter of grave concern.

You know.

The television show.

I have many friends who love the show, and I try to accept this, the way that I know many perfectly good, kind people enjoy mayonnaise on a sandwich, while others (me) would rather starve. Please don't think that I'm trying to claim any sort of intellectual high ground—I've watched way too many episodes of *The Love Boat* for that. I'm aware the TV Ingalls family provided years of wholesome G-rated entertainment, espoused fine values and warmed many cockles in many hearts, and that many fans of the Books also love the show, nonetheless—

Little House on the Prairie is not the same as *Little House on the Prairie*, which was only one of the Books anyway, and set in Kansas, not Minnesota, and even TV Walnut Grove wasn't in Walnut Grove, since the show was filmed in California.

The show premiered the same year I received the Books for my birthday (1974), but somehow I didn't hear about it for a few years. The news made me hyperventilate a little. I loved Laura. I loved TV.

Expectations for the convergence ran high. For my first viewing, I gathered all my stuffed animals (and the Books) and formed a horseshoe around the tube, the very picture of innocence and trust as I waited for my idol to come to life. Then the flutes toodled and all these kids tumbled down a grassy knoll.

From first flop I smelled trouble.

At first, the cast showed promise. Mary Ingalls was about right—pretty, blonde and bland. Ma looked acceptable as well with her bun and flaps of hair tucked modestly over her ears. As for Carrie, little girls are all pretty cute, so she wasn't of much importance. Nellie and Willie Oleson? Both on target. Willie, especially. That slack-jawed kid with the googly eyes was money.

From there it went... downhill.

Reverend Alden emerged from his church a cavefish, pale and jowly. Mr. Edwards? A grizzled disaster, nothing like the lean wildcat from Tennessee. The mere existence of a fabricated Doc Baker with his crinkled, crackpot brow was likewise a thorn, but while irritating, these minor leaguers weren't significant enough to cause much disturbance. Until—

Pa.

The real Charles Ingalls was a compact, stringy man with wild dark hair, bushy beard and twinkly blue eyes, not a pretty boy with curly locks, beefy buns and baby-faced jowls. TV Pa looked more suited for work as an aftershave model than life on the wild frontier. It was hard to take.

Even so I was hanging in there. I was a kid, and kids can be pretty determined when it comes to watching TV, but then—the Betrayal.

Laura.

Where do I start?

The freckles. There is never any mention of Laura having freckles. And TV Laura wasn't small enough to earn the nickname Half-Pint. Furthermore, she did not strike me as strong as a little French horse, nor as flutterbudgety. But while the physical details were disconcerting, the true treachery emerged as liberties were taken with Laura's character.

(1) Laura Ingalls—*not* a grinner.

Throughout the Books, Laura's eyes shine from time to time. She smiles, laughs out loud even, but she did not pull her lips back in a permanent, ingratiating suture, as if auditioning for a toothpaste commercial.

(2) Laura Ingalls—*not* a busybody.

TV Laura, when not grinning, was sticking her nose in other people's business and then whining when they told her to shut up and go away.

(3) Laura Ingalls—*not* a drama queen.

TV Laura was forever running and posturing and yelling. The real Laura did not flail her arms shouting "Pa! Pa!" like a crow with Tourette's. The real Laura had quiet talks with her Pa at night. The real Laura was stoic and faced disaster with a collected head.

At my freshman dorm in college, the residents had a drinking game based on the show. Every time someone cried, people took a shot. By hour's end, all of the residence hall was arm in arm, yodeling "Take Me Home, Country Roads."

(4) Laura Ingalls—*not* a crybaby.

I knew times were bad when I found myself rooting for Nellie. I secretly hoped that town girl would punch imposter Laura and send those buckteeth flying through the air like mah-jong tiles.

Now let's talk story. (If you need to replenish a beverage or take a bathroom break, this would be a good time.)

From the start, the high-handed moralizing and melodrama of the TV Ingalls family betrayed the spirit of the Books. Any moment a violin might screech as Mrs. Oleson bolted down Main Street, skirts flying while the menfolk stood flabbergasted by a pickle barrel. With all the histrionics and tragedy, how could anyone farm? Pioneers went to town for seed wheat and came back with rabies. The women wrung more hands than laundry. No one had chores, all people did was fall in love and adopt stray children, who littered the fields like prairie dogs.

Season after season the tragedy snowballed. Pretty soon it wasn't enough to have Mary go blind, so the whole town went blind. Then it was dull having everyone blind, so everyone's sight was restored. One would have thought the hardest-working man of the frontier was the town ophthalmologist. The show dragged on for so long

TV Laura puberized and met TV Almanzo, a blonde California heartthrob (real Almanzo—not blonde). Nellie, the show's one consistent entertainment, became a Jewish man's shiksa. Tamed by Old Testament hot lovin', even Nellie was no fun anymore. From there the frontier deteriorated into *One Life to Live* in petticoats. The show finale featured a triple wedding with some cows that turned out to be a dream sequence.

Okay, I made that last bit up.

Because for the *actual* final episode, in what can only be described in Kevorkian terms as a mercy killing, the writers—no kidding—blew up the town.

Through the years I have caught episodes here and there because those reruns are like mayonnaise—seemingly loved by everyone but me. Once I start I can't stop, the way a person polishes off an entire bag of stale pork rinds, but with every credit roll, I'm left with a sense of violation. One problem with any cinematic attempt is that while Laura's powers of description are integral and satisfying in the Books, watching someone take an hour to make bullets is not that interesting. The only director who might have been up to the task was Ingmar Bergman (see *Fanny and Alexander*). Mostly I suspect that Laura's internal world is so perfectly captured in print, I can't imagine experiencing her any other way. For me, the show has nothing to do with Laura Ingalls. My life as Laura Ingalls Wilder exists only in the Books. That show is something else, and I only mention it to lance the festering, calico boil.

And maybe to vent a little.

The End

The rub was that I probably wouldn't be standing here if not for the show. Laura did not even mention Walnut Grove by name in *Plum Creek*, calling it only "town," while the pilot episode of the show mentioned Walnut Grove seven times. Television was the force behind fans descending upon rural Minnesota, and a tourist attraction evolved as a result. I did, at least, have to thank the show for that.

Laura Central had a cluster of historic buildings behind the gift shop. There was an 1898 depot, a chapel, an onion-domed house, a sod house, a little red schoolhouse and a covered wagon. The buildings were tiny and close together, creating a minivillage. As I walked, I found myself getting back in a Laura groove, stopping to inspect a bridle or a wagon if I wanted, or moving on if I didn't. My quest always made more sense in motion.

The real Walnut Grove (originally Walnut Station), I learned, was plotted as a township only a few weeks before the Ingalls family arrived in spring of 1874. The first permanent settler was none other than the "good neighbor" from the Books, Mr. Eleck Nelson. Mr. Nelson was one of many Scandinavians who came to escape the strict social climate of their country. With the Dakota Indians recently evicted, Minnesota offered real estate opportunities. Scandinavians were probably well suited to the climate, coming as they did from countries with long, cold winters and midnight suns. I suspect Episcopalians never would have made it.

The museum had a display of Laura artifacts, including a quilt she had sewn and a Bible from the church the Ingalls family attended. The back room was dedicated to show memorabilia. There was a set of collectible plates, a board game, autographs from cast members and newspaper articles. A TV in the corner broadcasted reruns in perpetuity. TV Nellie was trashing her room in a raging hissy fit, hurling and smashing her toys.

"I hate you, Laura Ingalls! I HATE YOUUUUUU!" she screeched to the sound of organ chords inspired by Captain Nemo. Watching this tantrum made me suspect Courtney Love lifted a few moves from TV Nellie.

I averted my eyes and made my exit, leaving Nellie to her histrionics. Sometimes the sweetest victories against a nemesis are won by ignoring her presence.

About now it occurred to me I had neglected certain items in my greed spree: books. Back in the gift shop I snagged *The Little House Cookbook* (recipes for vanity cakes and Ma's sourdough biscuits!), *Free Land* by Rose Wilder Lane (fiction by Laura's daughter), *Farmer Boy* (so My Manly could read the story of his childhood) and then, on impulse, *Ghost in the Little House: A Life of Rose Wilder Lane* by William Holtz.

A young, blonde man of Nordic genetic stew rang me up. Last second I snagged a bottle of Laura Ingalls Wilder water from the cooler.

"The heat," I panted, pressing the water bottle to my cheek. "I'm dyin'. I'm from Alabama so you'd think I could take it."

"Hot in the summer. Cold in the winter. That's Minnesota!" he bragged.

"Sounds rough," I said.

"Oh, I'm not leaving. I'll die here." The cashier beamed, his broad, ruddy cheeks aglow.

In contrast to the Eeyore-style delivery of the Wilder Inn groundskeeper, the young man joyously proclaimed his fate. I thought it my duty to report that there are places in the country where people suffer only one season a year. I explained that in Alabama the summers are rough but the winters quite mild, while in Montana the winters are long but the summers glorious. My words, as all unsolicited advice, failed to impress. The young man's bubble cheeks went flat, as if wondering why anyone would want to go soft.

That late afternoon, from my room at the Wilder Inn, I could hear families organizing for the pageant. Car doors slammed, dads grumbled, moms double-checked for the camera and kids claimed they didn't need to go to the bathroom. I performed my little zipper dance and couldn't help but wonder if attending a family event without a family was a bit pathetic. I did, at least, have my copy of *Plum Creek* and Mr. Turtle, which I decided to bring with me. Not desperate, lonely or weird at all, right?

The pageant, due to copyright issues, was unable to quote the Books. This was, as you can imagine, upsetting news, but I braced myself in advance. *Fragments of a Dream*, I told myself, wasn't a performance of *Plum Creek* proper so much as a community celebration of local history. This was my chance to meet descendants of the good neighbor, Mr. Nelson. The pageant might not be strictly authentic Laura Ingalls Wilder, but it would be the real Walnut Grove, not some Hollywood concoction.

The air cooled as late afternoon became early evening. The pageant grounds hummed as attendees filtered in hauling totes, chairs and blankets. A permanent outdoor stage sat at the bottom of a grassy hill, creating a natural amphitheater. Families picnicked on the ground, and retirees layered up the hill in green, webbed folding chairs, the likes of which I had not seen since grilling hamburgers with my family in 1975. The multistaged set included a dugout with a spring, Oleson's Mercantile and a livery. Center stage the Pageant Singers, dressed in navy and khaki coordinates, performed Bob Seger's "Old Time Rock and Roll" in four-part harmony, crooning and snapping their fingers.

I stocked up on concessions and went to browse the souvenir stand. The Girl Scouts of the Peacepipe Council crowded around, clutching bonnets for purchase. The Marys waited patiently to pay while the Lauras already had them on.

"Are you a fan of the Books?" I asked a teenage Viking in blonde pigtails.

"Uh, my second-grade teacher read us the one about the bears."

"*Little House in the Big Woods*," I said.

"Yeah, that one."

"Nice bonnet," I said. It was a good one—lemon-yellow sprigged with tiny blue cornflowers.

She thanked me and ran off to ransack some Twizzlers.

I was learning that for Minnesotans, Laura Ingalls Wilder wasn't necessarily a lifelong obsession, but a local historical figure. Kids were taken here on field trips to pay homage just as I used to visit the home of Helen Keller in Alabama. I imagined adults attended the pageant because it was the local happening. Related community events included a pioneer festival, a pageant supper, a Laura and Nellie look-alike contest, a Jaycees fishing derby and an ecumenical worship service. These social gatherings were all well and good, but I worried that not enough people were reading. I had this idea that I should buy a zillion copies of *Plum Creek* and distribute them like Gideon Bibles.

I wandered the grounds, the pageant creating new issues concerning me, the blue-flowered elephant in the room. People were confused by my dress and so was I. The pageant actors had license to wander around in prairie clothes, but what was I doing? It's one matter to get a job as Cinderella on the Disney Cruise. Parents beg their children to go hug the lady in the big blue dress, who, if we think about it, is only some stranger everyone prays has been through the proper background check. Life as a freelancer is another story. Children would run up and ask if I was in the pageant, and when I said "no," they looked bewildered, disturbed even. Their faces went blank before they turned and slumped away, or bolted in terror.

So when the next little boy came up I replied, "Why, yes! I'm Helena Kindernoodle. I taught Laura how to make lindenberry tarts like in the old country."

Kids will believe anything, but I didn't sell my line to the parents, who hustled their little ones away. Apparently, I was the reason kids' faces appear on milk cartons. What I needed was a calico posse. Rappers would look ridiculous with gold teeth and droopy drawers if they didn't have twenty people surrounding them dressed the exact same way. But for all my trip planning (maps, reservations, advance tickets), I had neglected to arrange for an entourage. I had to go this alone.

I found a nice spot on the grass beside a mother with two girls dressed as Mary and Laura and set up camp. In addition to Mr. Turtle and *Plum Creek* I had thought to pack a hand-sewn, star pattern quilt from the Ozarks that my mother had given as a Christmas present. I thought about how Laura had eventually become an Ozark country farmwoman, crafting the handiwork I had seen that very afternoon at the museum. While leery of the dress, I discovered Minnesotans loved the quilt. I experienced a sudden flush of popularity, people asking whether I had sewn it, and where it was from. One girl in a green bonnet shyly walked up and said she thought my quilt was really pretty before blushing furiously and running away, which made me all mushy inside.

This must be said: little girls in bonnets are the best.

"Come on along! Come on along! Let me take you by the hand!" The Pageant Singers belted "Alexander's Ragtime Band" while I examined the twenty-six page brochure that gave thanks to everyone ranging from "Animal Handlers" to "Popcorn and Cleanup." The first pageant had been performed in 1978, at a Walnut Grove auditorium. Since then, the production had grown quite elaborate, with mechanized props, live animals and special effects, including simulated wheels of fire and a locust plague accurate enough to disgust me. The pageant had two acts, fifteen scenes and fifty-three actors. Two original songs, "Fragments of a Dream" and "Plum Creek Solitude," had been written and recorded by local artist Pam Steffen. Given the town population to cast ratio, most Walnut Grove residents must have been involved one way or another.

The sun was tipping good night over the trees when a wagon drawn by two horses made its way down and around the front of the stage. A pioneer family clambered out by the dugout to make a fresh start in Minnesota. The pageant consisted of a series of bucolic episodes based on *Plum Creek*, with certain additions, such as a town council scene. Sets transitioned from the church to Oleson's Mercantile to the dugout and back again, complex wooden mechanisms clicking and whirring giant props into place. The moon rose, and I found that as the sky darkened, I blended with the audience. In the dark we were all Laurafans hoping for a connection of some sort, either with Laura, or the past, or the people around us. Some kids splintered off and started a game of football off to the side. I had a strong urge to join them, but I was a big girl now, and too old to fidget. I sat patiently through the Union Congregational Church scene and waited for Nellie Oleson to get hers at the creek, the part where Laura lures her into the still water teeming with leeches. Every time Nellie took the stage, the entire audience booed with glee.

I saved Plum Creek for a postpageant day, hoping I could commune in peace, spend a little quality time with Laura away from the horde. The homesite was one and a half miles down from Walnut Grove on County Road 5, on the Gordon family farm. The Gordons, upon receiving the mandate that their farm is a holy site, have accepted their fate graciously. They allow visitors to regularly drive on their property and have even created a little park.

To the right of the red barn was a hand-painted sign and an honor system drop box for the money: $4 suggested donation per person, $20 per tour bus. As hoped, the site had emptied out. I drove in, parked the car in the shade and sat for a moment with the doors open, resting before going out in the roasting sun. Another car rolled up, slowed down to snap a photo and left.

Tourist attraction. Check.

The "wonderful house," the first frame house Charles Ingalls ever built with milled wood, no longer existed. The dugout home was also gone, collapsed sometime in the 1920s, but a footbridge crossed over Plum Creek, leading to a sign marking the original location. A dirt wallow remained, the worn area looking as though a very large animal had taken a very long nap. The prairie was up high, and I could envision how the excavated home would have been hidden from plain view when the Ingalls family first arrived, the only clue a stovepipe sticking out in the prairie. Squinting because of the intense glare, I stared across the prairie into the sun. I imagined runaway oxen and haystacks that *must stay stacked*. Over there, perhaps, once napped Johnny Johnson the Norwegian herder.

The Gordons had let a few acres go natural so Laurafans could experience a landscape besides cornfields. The prairie was bright and green with swaths of purple bee balm in bloom. White cloud puffs lounged in the soft blue sky. Even so, the Minnesota prairie was not pastoral. Insects and the birds that eat them screeched over a feeble breeze. The harsh sun was like shards of glass in my eyes, and I struggled with the heat. I had always seen the bonnet as a symbol of female domestication, but I discovered a practical purpose—nineteenth-century Ray-Bans. The fabric also protected my face, and the back flap kept me from growing red of neck. The downside was the bonnet functioned as blinders. The landscape was framed, limited. I could only move forward or turn my head like a periscope. I didn't care for the restriction and understood why Laura didn't either. We're not the confinement type. The strings chafing my neck were bad enough, but I couldn't stand being unable to see. Within a minute the bonnet hung down my back again.

Sorry, Ma.

A skirt on the prairie was another matter. Bloomers were probably more constricting than my bikini pants, but even still, I bet the ventilation was nice. The wide-open skirt stood up to the immense landscape, and I gave a little twirl à la Julie Andrews in *The Sound of Music*. Pants just wouldn't have been the same. I walked the mowed path, kicking my flounce as I went. With each step grasshoppers whirred, cracking like tiny popguns.

The grasshopper plague, of course, is the crisis of *Plum Creek*. When people roll their eyes and accuse the Books of presenting a Pollyanna version of pioneer life, I refer them to *Plum Creek*, Chapter Twenty-Five. One day Laura goes outside and sees a giant glittering cloud approaching. The sun is soon eclipsed. Insects fall like hail—only alive and crawling. Within hours the prairie and crops are ground to dust. In most children's books, grasshoppers are grandfatherly types who dispense sage advice and play classical music with their wings. Not on Laura's prairie. I bent down to study a little brown guy clinging to a blade of grass.

The Alabama grasshoppers I grew up with were black with an orange stripe down the back. They began tiny and numerous, whittling down to a few giant, lumbering beasts by summer's end, four to five inches long. These grotesques were what I had always imagined plopping down on Laura, but I was wrong. Laura's grasshoppers were, technically speaking, Rocky Mountain locusts (a locust is a grasshopper that swarms). The insect's cycle, unbeknownst to the settlers, was that every decade multitudes would hatch and catch an airstream east to feed. From 1873 to 1877, the Rocky Mountain locust devoured the Midwest, and Pa moved to Minnesota right in the worst of it. In 1875, the swarm measured 1,800 miles long and 180 miles wide. The locusts devastated the entire Great Plains that year, and the following two as well. Long term, though, the homesteaders would exact their revenge. The lush western valleys—the insects' breeding grounds—were plowed up and chewed by cattle. The Rocky Mountain locust is now extinct.

The path that connected the dugout hollow to Plum Creek had been worn slick by weekend pilgrims, so I had to skiddle-slide down. It was still hot down by the creek, but the shade provided some relief. Down and around I saw the waterway bend, trimmed by the green overhang of willows, plum thickets abounding with plump fruit. I gathered my skirts and squished my toes in the brown silt. The water turned cloudy as I walked until I held still and waited for the water to run clear again. A fallen white log spanned the creek. I waded over and sat, willing the air to gather force into a real breeze.

A creek is the perfect-sized playground for a young girl. Not too big and not too small. Tiny blue skippers sipped water from mud flats of wee beaches. Sticks in the water made Barbie rapids. I folded a few leaf boats and watched them float downstream, cheering them to overcome pebble blockades.

The locust plague might be the epic disaster of *Plum Creek*, but to me, the most terrifying moment in all the Books is the time Laura almost drowns. Disobeying a direct order from her parents, she goes to play after flooding rains have transformed the usually tranquil creek into a torrent. The rushing water almost sweeps her away. She finds herself struggling to survive, one arm desperately hooked around a wooden plank that spans the creek. Laura comes of age many times in the series, but this to me is one of the key moments, the moment she discovers her true mettle, when she learns that while there are forces stronger than her, that might even kill her, they cannot break her.

I personally experienced Laura's terror in Montana when a friend and I went tubing down the Blackfoot River. In complete ignorance, we put in twenty miles away from our second parked car. Six hours later, we realized we had traveled maybe a fourth of our intended distance, and that the curving river had carried us to remote wilderness. The glacial water that was bracing for the first hour turned cold, then miserable, before the setting sun made hypothermia a real possibility. We had seen no living creatures that day beyond giant beavers with piano key incisors. No one knew where we were.

Darkness descended on the canyon as we hit our hundredth series of rapids, but this time a boulder bumped me out of the tube. When the water engulfed me, pulling me under with terrifying strength, I instinctively knew that if I didn't get back to my little black donut, I was in serious jeopardy. If I hadn't been a competitive swimmer once, and known how to put down my head and *kick*, I don't know what would have happened.

Later, my friend confessed she thought that was the last of me: *Dixie Greenhorn Perishes in Montana River Adventure*. Like Laura, the power of the water shocked me. At the same time, I never doubted I would reach the tube. This was the brand of goal-oriented confidence that I wished I could access all the time, that Courtney Love brand of chutzpah where you go for what you want first, ask questions later.

Plum Creek is also the setting of Laura's revenge, the scene that gave the pageant audience such delight, when Laura lures Nellie into the leech-infested water. Other rival retributions take place in the Books, but this is the sweetest. The fictional character Nellie Oleson is in truth a composite of Laura's childhood nemeses (Nellie Owens, Genevieve Masters and Stella Gilbert). This merging of three characters makes for better storytelling, but I see a greater truth in the device, in that whenever I encounter a new rival, it feels like the same one turning up again.

I'd had more than one Nellie in my life as well. Tammy Cochran from swim team who waved her blue ribbons in my face, screaming, "I beat you! I beat you!" Tonya Platt, the terror of Bus 89, who grabbed my journal and read it aloud. There was Candy Barton from band, who squeaked her clarinet in my ear on purpose, and Joe Ann Whitbread, who thought she could read faster than me. As if. I grew older, and it seemed there was always a Prissy with size four Guess jeans, or a Didi stealing the affections of my true love. There were boy rivals, too. Greg Herman, know-it-all who punched me in the stomach. Naveen Patel, who told me the first story I wrote was "insipid." During my restaurant career, about once a year, some restaurant customer would get in my face, screaming that he (it was always a man) would get me one day, demanding I "give him my name."

All this dredging up of past rivals had riled me up. Charged, I picked up a huge stick and swung it like a baseball bat against a tree. Whack! It cracked in a satisfying snap. I checked behind me, expecting Amish tourists in a minivan, but I was alone.

That night I sprung for the Valentine Inn, a large, pink Victorian house replete with columns, bay windows and a wraparound porch. Suitcase in hand, I knocked on the door like an estranged relative. Proprietress Sis Beierman answered, a tidy woman with short, blonde hair, shrouded in an afghan. She apologized that she was sick and covered her mouth. I registered and saw I was the only guest; post pageant the town had cleared out. Mrs. Beierman showed me to my room, apologized again, and retreated to her separate residence off to the side.

I selected a piece of white wicker furniture on the porch. As the evening sky turned silver and mauve, I watched kids ride their bicycles, the *E.T.* gang minus the alien. They frenetically pedaled down the street and back again, down and back again, not unlike pacing mental ward patients. Without crops to protect or cows to tend, they applied their energy to laps. I wondered if they were bored the way I had been as a child, questioning why they had been put on this earth. *I didn't ask to be born.*

After the kids were called home, the streets became eerily quiet. I stared at the power lines for a while, but really, there was nothing to do but try and go to bed. The house was dark and still, and I became conscious of sleeping alone in this large two-story house. There was an entire upstairs with the grander quarters. Earlier, I had snuck up there to explore and see how the other half lives (the other half has settees), before I slunk back down. I passed the staircase on the way to my room, concerned about all that empty, uninhabited space. It'd be easy for a person to hide up there. With a hatchet.

Muggings. Drive-bys. Random crime has never scared me, even though my Durham neighborhood was a regular feature on the local news. What makes me shake through the night is the Truman Capote, *In Cold Blood* kind of evil. The Clutters lived in what should have been the safest place in the world: small-town America. Then these psychos broke in and brutally murdered them. One moment young Nancy Clutter was teaching a young neighbor how to bake a pie, the next she was shot in her bed, and because of the isolation, no one could hear the screams. The boonies are where the truly grisly crimes happen. That's why horror movies—*Children of the Corn, Friday the 13th, The Shining*—are always set there.

I hated to break it to Mrs. Beierman, but her quaint, delightful bed and breakfast was a prime setting for murder. *Helena Bjorg did it with a Fabergé Egg in the white wrought iron daybed.*

My room was maroon and pink, decorated in a high Victorian

style, which did little to comfort me. Victorians were infamous for drugging women with laudanum and then stabbing their eyes out with stiletto letter openers. I couldn't help but wonder, what with all the Scandinavian immigrants, why Walnut Grove couldn't go for the IKEA aesthetic—it's harder for serial killers to hide amidst sleek modern furnishings. The giant hutches, armoires and dressers did little to quell my fears. Neither did the shelves packed with pallid, antique china dolls staring at me, one thousand Brides of Chucky. I huddled in my fluffy comforter against my fluffy pillow, thinking all the down could absorb a sharp blade.

I needed distraction. Pa's Big Green Book or a copy of *Milbank* weren't handy, so I pulled out one of my recent purchases, *Ghost in the Little House: A Life of Rose Wilder Lane*, by William Holtz. The gray cover was of Laura's daughter in a dark suit, her expression resembling Edgar Allen Poe's Annabel Lee, exhumed from her sepulcher by the sea. I knew the basics of Rose's story, that she had been the successful author before her mother, publishing stories, essays and novels for a living. A quick scan revealed that Rose had been quite an amazing woman, leaving her small hometown in Missouri to travel the world over.

Ghost in the Little House began by acknowledging that any biography of Rose was going to have to live in the shadow of her more famous mother—as a "ghost" one might say. *Yawn*, I thought. This didn't strike me as any big revelation, but a few pages in, hairs prickled on the back of my neck. Holtz knew how to present his information in the ever-reasoned tone of an academic, but darkness lurked beneath the suede elbow-patched exterior.

Page four Holtz dropped the pretense of civility: "Laura Ingalls tried and failed."

Holtz went on to describe Laura the failure. As a farmer, primarily, but there was more—Laura had failed as a writer. Holtz meant *ghost* as in *ghost*writer; meaning Laura didn't write the Books. Her daughter did. Rose had been, after all, the first successful writer in the family and was known to have ghostwritten projects.

I flipped to the back so I could stand down my accuser. The photo showed Dr. Holtz in his office, legs crossed, sitting behind a copy of *David Copperfield*. He wore the requisite English professor garb: khakis, crewneck sweater and black-rimmed glasses dangling around his neck. His crepey eyes stared dourly outward, his lips a hyphen. *What's your freaking problem?* I asked Dr. Holtz. As adults we all learn that Santa Claus and the Tooth Fairy are fictions. We come to understand that Narnia and Hogwarts aren't real places, but in a world of anthrax and Armageddon, we had Laura Ingalls, our real-life heroine. Not anymore.

I was aware that the Books, although based in historical fact, had been published as works of fiction. Through *Laura Ingalls Wilder: A Biography*, by William Anderson, I had learned that Laura the author altered chronologies, compressed timelines, created composite characters (such as Nellie) and, in the case of Burr Oak, Iowa, left out one place she lived while growing up. None of that bothered me, because there was something so essentially true about the stories, Laura the character and her family, that my faith in Laura the person had always been absolute.

Until now.

Thanks, Dr. Feelbad.

The night wasn't going very well—I believe the technical description of my mood would be creeped out and depressed. I had lost interest in reading but was scared to get up and walk around for fear of smashing some valuable antique. I couldn't fall asleep because the baby dolls were waiting to come to life and stab me in the neck, after which, a serial killer was going to break in, tie me up, drag me to the basement and shoot me.

I sighed, closed the book and took one last look at the cover. Something about this Laura exposé was off. I didn't know what, but I had also read the entire *Encyclopedia Brown* series, so I was going to sleuth it out. I should have known that growing up, even a second time, couldn't take place without a few obstacles. I was midway through the series now and about to leave the little girl days behind. It made sense that from here on out I would have to juggle adult complexities, such as reconciling Laura the person with Laura the fictional character. For now, it was too late to fix the world, and my mind churned like a Plum Creek freshet. I needed rest.

Professor Crankytweed could wait. I put him down on the nightstand. Next, I stared down the dolls, informing them if they tried anything I'd go Nellie/Courtney on them. Perhaps they were familiar with Courtney's kinderwhore look that featured severed baby doll heads, because that shut them up. The serial killer, I consoled myself, was most likely in Texas that night. They usually were. Calmed now and ready to sleep, I pulled the string on the lacy lamp and embraced the dark.

I awoke ready to move on. I'd had enough insects, rivals and serial killers. But first, breakfast. Most mornings I stumble around with a pot of coffee, but I rallied for the cause. The formal dining table was overkill for one guest, so Mrs. Beierman and I sat at the counter as we watched *The Today Show*. She handed me a mug of rich, dark coffee with full whipping cream.

Mrs. Beierman whisked our eggs with authority. When they were frothy, she set the bowl down and vigorously scooped a football of butter in the skillet. *Thwack!* Take *that*, American Heart Association. We talked about her small-town life, working at the floral shop during the day, hunting with her Hungarian Visla in the fall and running this bed and breakfast, trying to make a little extra income. The high-strung sepia-colored dog pattered and paced around the kitchen, nails tip-tapping on the floor.

"Did you ever read the Books?" I couldn't help but ask.

"No, I never did," she admitted. "You know, they are big in Japan. It's how they learn American history. Not so long ago a huge group came through. I was featured once in a Japanese travel magazine. And they love that show."

"Oh," I said.

"I know," she said, shaking her head. "Filmed out in California! It looks nothing like Minnesota. All those mountains." She picked up the bowl and beat with renewed, furious vigor, eggs foaming to the cusp of meringue.

Before I left I wanted to see if I could extract one more piece of information. I admit I baited Mrs. Beierman a little bit, keeping the conversation on funeral bouquets a little longer than necessary. I learned she was a grandmother (news that surprised me), but a ways from retirement.

"Do you think you might retire somewhere else?"

"Oh, no," she said. On TV, Willard Scott grinned and waved. Willard Scott: Grinner. Proprietor of Valentine Inn: Not a grinner. "I guess I'll die here."

Mrs. Beierman froze for a second and stared off into space. Then, with a quick shake of the head, she sprang back into motion, pouring our eggs into the sizzling pool of fat. Yellow ribbons curled into flapping wings, and I have to say, since that morning I have not been able to return to a light spray of olive oil.

I would die someday, but not in Minnesota. I was ready to head west, move to higher ground, make a fresh start, cool off in the driving winds. A few miles out Highway 14, a family of wild turkeys scuttled across the road. I thought of the Visla, like Jack, joyfully running to fetch and bring one back to his mistress, her sure, brisk hands dressing the bird for dinner. The morning sky brightened past coral to soft lemon. Heat creeped along the horizon, reminding me of the need to push on.

I removed Hole from the CD player. "Teenage Whore" was too much this early in the day. But I'd be back. I like to believe there's a bit of Courtney Love inside of me, the part who is driven, ruthless and cunning. Sometimes I need a rival to challenge me. Without Tammy Cochran flaunting her blue ribbons in my face, maybe I never would have pushed myself at swim practice, and would have drowned in the Blackfoot River. If Naveen Patel had never described my writing as "insipid," I might not have been driven to prove him wrong. That's why Hole is the music I turn to when I need to kick ass.

"My goodness!" said Mary. "I could never be as mean as that Nellie Oleson."

Laura thought: "I could. I could be meaner to her than she is to us, if Ma and Pa would let me."

CHAPTER SIX
LITTLE HOUSE IN THE SUBURBS

Tuscaloosa, Alabama
Durham, North Carolina
Frontier Valley, Montana

*I feel like I'm growing up a lot here because, like, before, like, if
I was in Temecula or California or wherever I used to live, like,
I wouldn't do anything. I would just sit on my butt and watch
TV, and I was just a lazy person. But, like, now that I'm
actually doing work I feel like a better person. Like, you know,
I'm actually doing something to help other people.*
—Tracy Clune, *Frontier House*

For a time I had the goal of writing my life story for children Little
House–style. My idea was to update the Books for a modern age,
but keep the simplicity, the wholesomeness, and convey that same
deep sense of family security.

Little House in the Suburbs
By Kelly Kathleen Ferguson
   Once upon a time, thirty-five years ago, a little girl
lived in the Big Suburbs of Alabama, in a little ranch
house made of brick. Great pine trees stood all
around, with vast green lawn in between. Beyond were
more pine trees, and more lawns. As far as a person
could go there were ranch brick houses and pine trees
and lawns. There were no restaurants. There were no
shops. There were no people with melanin. There were
only cul-de-sacs, and pine trees and lawns, and the

70

people and the animals that had their houses among them.

Dogs lived in the Big Suburbs, and tabby cats, and hamsters. Gray squirrels scrambled up and down the pine trees. Toads and bunnies hopped in the yards. Bugs—grasshoppers, fleas, mosquitoes and cockroaches—were everywhere...

It wasn't long before I ran into problems. The Big Suburbs didn't create the same feeling of isolation as the Big Woods, while tabby cats and hamsters did little to create an atmosphere of peril. Fleas didn't exactly count as wildlife. The suburbs were remote, but there was no need to lay in winter supplies, not with ready access to Winn Dixie.

Yet I persevered. My hope was that I could rescue my story through delectation in the details. Laura the writer always was the mack daddy of minutiae. Her early books don't have much plot, yet the writing holds our interest. That's because Laura knew better than to tersely report, "Ma made the butter." No, she catalogued the process with exacting care: the churn, the wooden churn-dash, the wooden churn-cover, the grainy milk, the grains, the golden lump, the buttermilk, the butter mold and the golden little butter pats with the strawberry and its two leaves on top. I deduced that I could also create a satisfying read by recreating nostalgic experiences in great detail. We all love to sit around and remember the knickknacks, foods and fashions of bygone eras. The seventies had plenty to draw upon there. Mom's index cards of Crock-Pot recipes alone were ripe for the picking.

Little House in the Suburbs: Take Two

Ma was in the kitchen next to the gleaming avocado appliances. She was so pretty with her purple paisley scarf tied around her head. She smiled at Kelly.

"Why don't we make Pa a treat?"

First, Ma took out some green butter pickles and chopped them fine. Then she opened a can of tuna fish and emptied it into the robin's-egg-blue Tupperware bowl. With her plastic spatula Ma didn't miss a flake of that delicious, pale meat. Ma took a jar from the fridge and mixed in white creamy mayonnaise. Last she added the chopped pickles, a sprinkle of salt and a few shakes of Accent seasoning. This would be tuna salad for lunch...

Problem number two: The seventies weren't that long ago, and the rituals of my childhood weren't so different from today. I tried to explain how we did things "back in the day." I conjured relics—the rotary phone, orange mushroom canisters, ponchos—but in those details I failed to capture the tiny joys of my childhood. The litany read more like a joke. Even still I wrote on, convinced I could, with consistent, applied effort, channel something of Laura's magic. Then I reached my literary Waterloo:

> "Wait," Ma said. "I've got another little surprise."
> From the pantry she pulled out a box of Ritz crackers and a tiny silver tin of deviled Spam.
> "Why, nothing beats Ma's Spam on a Ritz cracker!"
> Pa exclaimed. "You treat a man to a feast, Diana!"

Disaster. I had dissolved into parody.

The tragic flaw of *Little House in the Suburbs* was that my story had no high stakes. When Laura marvels over each section of an orange, we the readers understand that food wasn't always plentiful. Before Ben Woodworth's birthday party, she had never *seen* an orange. That kind of wonder can only come from a place of deprivation. Laura battled disease, prairie fire, blizzards and wolves. My greatest childhood threat was ennui. I was crying all the time and didn't know what I was crying about. A whimpering child makes for a lousy heroine.

A folder exists on my computer desktop called "Writing R.I.P." And that's where a slim, incomplete volume of *Little House in the Suburbs* remains, and shall remain, forever.

It wasn't long after that I discovered why my first attempt at memoir failed.

When I lived in Durham, a couple I knew hosted *Sex and the City* parties. A small group of us convened weekly for booze, bawdy humor and treats.

"Another Sunday splash m'dear?" Friedrich would murmur, not waiting for my answer as he topped off my glass with New Zealand Sauvignon Blanc. His husband, William, worked behind the scenes, refilling tiny bowls of noshables and serving up plates of hors d'oeuvres.

We all loved Sundays.

One week, Friedy's usually sunny expression was clouded over. He had bad news.

"No *Sex and the City* this week, but we've recorded this… well… it's a Public Television reality show called *Frontier House*. I hope you don't mind."

He seemed a bit sheepish at his offer of educational programming, but our group consensus took about half a second. Why should a little learning interfere with wine and snacks? Within moments we assumed our usual seats. I curled up on the forest green loveseat, and Friedy cued up the video entertainment.

Onscreen three families in prairie garb walked across a breathtaking landscape of rolling prairie, snowcapped peaks and azure sky. Cut. A teenage girl with a scythe harvested hay. Cut. Another girl led a cow out to pasture. Cut. A man hitched up horses to a covered wagon. The voice-over explained that *Frontier House* gave three modern-day American families a claim out West to prove up. After a brief training with historical experts, the families went "back in time," to 1883, where they would sacrifice all modern conveniences to live as pioneers did in the nineteenth century. The test: could they make it?

Whoa.

Hold the mixed nuts.

Hold the New Zealand Sauvignon Blanc.

Hold, even, the Medjool dates stuffed with Stilton wrapped in bacon.

Starstruck, I staggered up to the screen and sat on the floor, my nose inches from the glass. I could hear the echo of my mother's voice, "You need to back up or you'll get cancer!" Premature death was the calculated risk I was willing to take. Everyone else seemed to miss *Sex and the City*, but hours later I remained glued to the set, transfixed. Friedrich tiptoed up and touched my shoulder.

"You okay, sweetums?"

The camera panned out to the craggy Rocky Mountains shimmering in silhouette. I went woozy.

"Honey?" Friedrich repeated, concern edging into his voice.

"*There*," I intoned, pointing. "I want to *go there*."

Friedy gave me little pat and refilled my glass.

"WHERE?" I demanded, still pointing. I was so agog I had neglected to pay attention.

"Oh, let's see if I can remember. Utah?"

"Montana," piped in William.

Montana.

There. I wanted to go there.

And eventually, I did.

I became addicted to *Frontier House*—the crops, the big sky, the hand-baked breads, the livestock. I watched and waged internal debates over how I would fare without modern conveniences. The thought of giving up telephones and laptops had a great appeal. No tampons or ibuprofen? Eh. I turned these pros and cons over and over in my mind, but while my capacity for wondering what pioneer life would "really" be like was endless, what fascinated me the most was the dynamics of the adults versus the children.

Going in the summer, the adults were rarin' to go, anxious to prove their mettle. After all, they had applied for this television show, hoping to be selected from a competitive pool of five thousand families. The kids? Not so psyched. They were dragged along, convinced that abandoning the twentieth century was an idiotic move. The more the reality of the situation sunk in (no toilet paper, no cheeseburgers), the more they balked. *Are you kidding me?* their faces telegraphed. *This is my summer vacation?* They kvetched and sniveled. The teenage girls sneaked in makeup, and the boys bellyached about their video games. When it came time to head up the wagons and travel to the homestead, the children followed as if marching the Trail of Tears.

At the end of that first day, nine-year-old Conor Clune wailed before a camera about the "worst day" of his life, which meant (1) he fell out of the wagon, (2) he lost his worm while fishing with not even a bite, and (3) a dog mouthed his leg (he called this "attacked by a vicious dog"). Admittedly, the wagon horses running away had been scary, and the incident could have been serious, but I couldn't help thinking the kid needed to buck up. Whiny, sensitive and easily discouraged—Conor reminded me of myself at his age. I remember the days when the wrong potato chips or a boo-boo caused a major meltdown. That's what these kids seemed like, their characters the texture of instant potatoes. During a surprise snow, the teenage girls had to go out and milk the cow. The hike was long and cold, and their socks got wet, but the situation didn't warrant hysteria. The girls demonstrated all the mettle of the little piggy that cried "wee, wee, wee" all the way home.

But get this. Over the course of the program, the adults and kids experienced a role reversal. It wasn't long before the romance of "going back in time" wore off for the grown-ups, who grew increasingly petty and short-tempered over the lack of modern comforts. The Clunes griped about their absent sex life while the Glenns found themselves on the brink of divorce. Two of the three families (the adults) became out-and-out cutthroat; each determined to "win" at homesteading as they counted chicken eggs and compared the rise of their sourdough biscuits.

"Two-thirds of the people didn't make it out here. Well, you do the math. And I can tell you we're the family that's going to make it," snapped Karen Glenn, a scrappy woman from Tennessee who spent the summer churning butter like Rocky training for the rematch.

The third family, a young couple, kept out of the fray. They fared a little better, I believe, because they kept their sense of humor about the privations of nineteenth-century life. They giggled and sang and goofed with the camera. Kristen Brooks struggled one morning to make a pancake over an open flame and rolled her eyes at the camera, her curly hair unwashed and wild.

"It sucks! It just totally sucks! It's totally hard out here," she said, but at least she could laugh as she scraped her giant, doughy mess from the skillet.

One could argue that the young couple had it easier because they were free from the burden of having kids, except the kids didn't seem to be the problem. While the first few weeks in Frontier Valley were a whinefest of major proportions, once the kids let go, they adapted. No, wait. They *thrived*. Erinn Patton, a twelve-year-old, turned out to be a regular Almanzo Wilder with livestock; the cows blossomed under her care. She wasn't tending to the animals so she could "win," but for the sake of tending to the animals. The teenage girls went out and got to work in the field. Conor learned to hunt with a bow and arrow. While the parents bellyached and squabbled, the kids developed a zenlike attention to their jobs—jaws set, eyes focused on the task at hand.

The farm cure. It was real.

At this point I would like to digress for a story from my Durham days that will, I hope, convey my mental state of existence for the twenty years before I moved West. My intention is to show how a child of indecision became a Generation X, directionless adult, trapped in a mire of circular thinking. This story is in many ways a random selection, but it should work as a representation of all the other stories that end with me a saltwater blob of tears, most of which I have thankfully blocked out.

Chocolate Cake. Coconut Cake.

One night, at the last restaurant I worked at, a customer ordered our restaurant's signature coconut cake. This should have been a straightforward event where a customer said, "I would enjoy the coconut cake, please," and I replied, "Excellent choice. It is delicious." After this my job would be to serve the cake so the customer could enjoy it, after which I tell her I am glad she enjoyed it.

This was my job. A simple job.

The restaurant also had a signature *chocolate cake* on the menu, one of those decadent, pudding creations made with Scharffen Berger, an elite California brand that sources the best cacao in the world and employs artisan methods. This made it expensive. The cake had to be baked to order. This took time. The *coconut cake* was expensive as well, but could be served immediately.

This particular night my coconut cake seemed to be taking a long time, since preparation only meant plating, but rule one of serving is Do Not Hound the Kitchen. This was one of those crazy busy nights, and unless I wanted a cleaver in my forehead by way of reply, it was best to let those handling sharp knives alone. Fifteen minutes later a chocolate cake appeared in the server window. I picked up the ticket. My name was on it.

"Uh, Billy," I said. "I made a mistake."

I got a look, but amiably enough, he slung us servers the chocolate cake and swiftly plated a coconut cake for me.

Later, another customer ordered a coconut cake and (after fifteen minutes), another chocolate cake came up in the window. Again, my name was on the ticket. As much as I wanted to believe the computer had been hijacked by an alien virus, I had to face the obvious—I had rung in the wrong cake. A second time. Billy replated the correct cake, this time less amiably.

"Awesome, Kelly," said the garbage disposal waiter, efficiently spooning rich chocolate cake in his mouth as he prepared coffee. "Why don't you mess up a filet next time?"

The third time Billy threw the chocolate cake in the trash with a slap.

Then I needed a chocolate cake. I waited the appropriate amount of time. And waited. The chocolate cake always took a while, but even so, my order shouldn't have taken this long. There was no way that I could ask about it either. No way. Feigning casual interest, my nerves razors, I peered around the corner.

"Hey," Billy said. "Are you going to pick this up?"

There, in the sugary gallows of the pastry station, sat a wilted coconut cake.

"Of course!" I said, whisking it away and running to the computer to ring in a chocolate cake, avoiding the stares of my customers who by this point must have all been wondering what it was with cake in this restaurant. I don't know what happened that night. I wish I did. All I know is that every time a person asked for a dessert menu, my innards turned to brick.

Coconut cake. Chocolate cake. Coconut cake. Chocolate cake.

Sometimes I was able to pull a little switcharoo, but as the mistakes piled up, I began running out of options. I could smell I was on the verge of a stern office chat. I had suffered many stern office chats over the years where the manager asked, "What do you suggest we do about this?" or, more to the point, "Perhaps it's time you moved on." I didn't think I could take another one. I was one office chat away from the gossamer film that was my self-confidence disintegrating. Somehow, I had to conceal my errors from management, my fellow waitstaff, the kitchen *and* my customers. I determined that if I rang in one of each cake, then I could make good with the customer, who wouldn't have to wait half an hour for dessert. Then I covered my tracks by sneaking in the bathroom and flushing the mistake down the toilet. To avoid the extra dessert showing up on the bill, I split the wrong cake off to a pretend check on the computer, which I then closed out to cash—costing me $8.50 each time.

At the end of a shift that put me fifty dollars in the red, I approached the manager with my trembling hand steadied around a goblet of red wine and casually suggested that maybe we could call the coconut cake "white cake," or something easier to read.

"Why?" she said, not even looking up from her paperwork. "It's so obvious. Just read the button."

She was right. A normal person did not disintegrate into a dysfunctional, quaking mess over a simple task. A normal person went to a computer and pushed a button. My childhood puttering around the cul-de-sac had followed me into adulthood.

What kind of person is so useless she can't ring in a piece of cake?

Young Logan Patton's coming of age came fast and sure in Frontier Valley when it was time to butcher the hog. When first told the bad news, he followed his mother around protesting the fate of "JoJo Pumpkin," but no Charlotte the spider arrived to rescue this pig. After the kill, Logan was changed, lean and tough, a hardened glint in his eye.

"Every animal that's raised is going to be killed. That's just how life is, basically, if you think about it," he philosophized.

I bet fresh pork was tasty after weeks of cornbread and beans, but it came with a price. Pork no longer came from the grocery store. Pork was meat.

It was while watching the children of *Frontier House* evolve that I came to understand the quivery beast inside me. All my childhood I had felt useless. Logan and the gang were necessary; running the farm was a full-time job. The girls had to milk the cow or there was no milk. Not only that, the cow was a huge family investment. Being in charge of the cow was a big deal. I wasn't allowed to touch anything worth more than five dollars. Desperate to get my hands on items of value, I would rifle through Mom's jewelry box or finger Dad's change on his dresser. Then I got in trouble.

It seems unrealistic that a modern child could ever delight over a used fur muff and a few oyster crackers for Christmas the way Laura did. I know that if Santa had brought me nothing but a penny, a tin cup and a heart-shaped cake, I would have hurled these items at my parents and run off in tears shouting, "I wish I was dead!" Here was another *Frontier House* miracle: Once the kids had actual responsibilities, and isolation from all the twentieth-century "stuff," their need for material goods evaporated. The girls no longer lived to primp. The boys no longer cared about video games. I had always thought my parents ruined my life because they didn't buy me enough Ralph Lauren Polo shirts in ninth grade, but maybe what I needed was a paradigm shift. My weak suburban ass needed to learn where meat came from. If I had, maybe I would have become an adult who could confidently order a piece of cake without melting down in crisis.

That was the crazy miracle I witnessed. The *Frontier House* kids forced to live like Laura became more like Laura—more capable, more resilient, the high-pitched tone easing out of their voices. They read books for recreation and developed an appreciation, nay, genuine thrill over the simple joys. There was a scene where Logan received an orange, his first piece of fruit in weeks, similar to Laura's experience at Ben Woodworth's birthday party. That boy tore into that fresh fruit with a vigor that would make a modern mother pass out from shock. A month into the summer, the children attended a one-room school. Initially skeptical of the cornball atmosphere, they soon came to love spelling bees and singing "Polly Wolly Doodle."

I repeat, modern teenage girls happily sang "Polly Wolly Doodle."

I am aware that as a product of the middle class, it is easy for me to go all Thoreau about our lives of quiet desperation. Memoirists Debra Marquart (*The Horizontal World: Growing Up Wild in the Middle of Nowhere*) and Judy Blunt (*Breaking Clean*) have told the stories of their lives as modern-day "Lauras" growing up on Great Plains farms. While I lay prostrate on my pink ruffled bedspread, reading about the sugaring off dance, these women gutted chickens and chopped ice off cows. Both authors dryly crack about how their farmhouses were no *Little House on the Prairie*. On *Frontier House*, the women and kids made the same comment more than once. "Trust me," Adrienne Clune said to the camera, wiping the grime off her brow, "This is no *Little House on the Prairie*," each word dripping with bile. (Although I suspect they mean the show? I can't help but notice none of these women blame, say, *On the Banks of Plum Creek*.)

I'm not saying that soon as a kid can reach the gear shift of a combine he should git out and git workin'. Children should keep their limbs and have enough to eat, but maybe kids need a sense of where their food comes from and a connection (dare I say) with nature. And perhaps children need a way to contribute to their families. If *Frontier House* was any indication, children are not only highly capable when given the chance, but superior to adults in their ability to adapt. I'm not sure how anyone would practically implement this strategy, although the recent trends of community and school gardens strike me as one possibility. I only know what I saw in Frontier Valley, and that the case study compelled me.

In the final segment of *Frontier House*, the families were back at their regular lives, settled back in their suburban homes, where pork meant Oscar Mayer wieners in the fridge. The adults appeared vaguely confused, as if they couldn't quite remember what all that pioneer mess was about. They squinted and stared into the middle distance. *Yeah*, their expressions read, *that was one crazy summer, living like hippies.*

80

The kids were another story. They were haunted, unable to recover. The teenage girls, reunited with their lip gloss, stood listlessly in the hot tub of the Clunes' mansion.

"Every day I always say I'm bored, and my parents get mad at me for it. There is nothing to do," Tracy Clune said.

"Basically it's really boring and you have to make it fun for yourself, I guess," Aine Clune concurred.

Logan was back at his video games. He sat, shoulders hunched, pushing buttons as the screen blipped and beeped. His eyes were fixed on the screen, lights flickering zombie white across his stricken, hollow face.

CHAPTER SEVEN
COMING OF AGE IN SUBURBIA

Tracy, South Dakota:
By the Shores of Silver Lake

A nineteenth-century train rolled on the horizon, a big black engine hauling a ghost load to nowhere. The Wheels Across the Prairie Museum was closed, but No. 9 stood guard, the wide, flaring smokestack reaching into the sky. I imagined smoke pouring out, the clickety-clack of wheels, the long whistle as the dark beast lurched to a stop.

In 1879, Tracy, Minnesota, marked the end of the line. It was here Ma, Mary, Laura, Carrie and Baby Grace, disembarked to meet Pa at the hotel. From Tracy they traveled by wagon to a railroad camp near Brookings, South Dakota. Once Pa earned some money working as a railroad paymaster, the plan was to file a claim further west in the Dakota Territory. The Homestead Act of 1862 promised 160 acres of open plains on a first-come, first-served basis. If a farmer lasted five years, he (or she, single women could file) received the deed to the property. Charles Ingalls was one of the hopeful.

The Ingalls family's fate, as all homesteaders, was linked with that of the railroads. Meteorological lore of the day claimed that "rain followed the plow," although more truthful was the plow followed the rails. Farmers depended on the railroad, for there was no point in harvesting a crop without a way to ship it, and they needed supplies from the East—coal, seed and tools. Of the 285 towns built between 1878 and 1889 in South Dakota, 182 were railroad towns. Railroads, in turn, needed farmers for their customer base. They advertised aggressively, luring settlers with promises of fertile lands and crops that sprung like magic beans from the rich, black earth. Wishing Trains traveled the Midwest, moving museums that displayed lavish spectacles of goods ranging from wheat sheaths to Rocky Mountain bighorn sheep to pineapples. They must have made for a good show. The population of the Dakotas grew from 12,000 in 1860, to 82,000 in 1870, to 249,000 in 1880, in what came to be known as the Great Dakota Boom. The Ingalls family was right in the thick of it.

I stood in front of No. 9 and pictured Ma and her girls traveling in their Sunday best, Ma so pretty in her dark delaine with white lace collar and cuffs. As a kid, the word *delaine* was mysterious to me, conjuring a glamour I could only hope to understand one day (a delaine is a fine wool). All I knew was Ma's best dress from the Big Woods sugaring off dance had been resurrected for this grand occasion, the family's first train ride.

In 1979, my family approached travel with a similar solemnity for our first airplane flight to Disney World. This vacation symbolized my parents' arrival in the middle class—Mickey Mouse the totem animal in this transition ceremony. For weeks we prepared, my mother nervously making lists, checking and rechecking for the tickets. Our wardrobes were carefully folded and belted in hard luggage (Samsonite, powder blue). The night before, we laid out our travel outfits and set three alarms. In the dark dream world of predawn, I donned my pressed chino skirt and white blouse, Mom fussing with the Peter Pan collar. At the airport women wore fine dresses with pantyhose and men, suits. Parents gripped their scrubbed children firmly by the hand. Flight attendants and pilots, Barbies and Kens brought to life, strutted by on their way to worldly destinations.

"Nowadays," I heard an older southern woman drawl recently at the Birmingham airport, one eyebrow arched, "everyone dresses like they ah headed for the *poooool*."

I saw her point. In front of us, a teenage girl's butt proclaimed itself JUICY. Most people lounging around the gate wore some version of tracksuits and ratty sneakers. I found myself longing for Audrey Hepburn to come clacking down the linoleum draped in Givenchy.

At the Tracy depot, I don't know that I was so pretty in my turquoise blue-flowered cotton after days in a car, but I did my best not to fidget. Reflecting on Ma's delaine, I realized my dress had yet another purpose—to commemorate the occasion of my journey. I thought of Laura helping Mary, who was blind now from fever, up the tall steps of the train, Carrie's eyes wide and fearful. During my stay in Minnesota, I had driven the seven-and-a-half-mile trip back and forth between Walnut Grove and Tracy multiple times in search of food or gas. Laura made this trip once, in one direction. When the Ingalls family moved, they packed everything a wagon could hold and traveled to a place sight unseen, putting their faith into the unknown.

West for Laura meant new. The West was new for me as well, and through my travels, I sought metaphor. An American trope, sure, but I suspected the power of belief was working. I was unstuck. Going west was by far the most at home and productive I had ever felt. Living in the West had been pretty great, too, but not as great as *going* west.

The only way to understand the differences between Minnesota, Kansas and South Dakota prairies is by travel close to the ground. You have to watch the soft hills shift in the skyline and rub the sun-cured grasses. That's because prairies aren't a biome, but an experience. To know it you have to live it. But just as Laura took on the responsibility of describing the landscape change to her blind sister, I will do my best.

Western Minnesota and De Smet lie east of the 100th meridian, the traditional dividing line between Midwest and West described by Wallace Stegner as "an inflexible line of aridity," but I perceived a distinct change at the 95th. The atmosphere went light. The sun was bright but not glaring, and my facial muscles relaxed. I was taken back to the South Dakota gas station, when my skin went matte, the moment "West began." Green prairie turned gold. The clusters of trees thinned out until "tree" became a monument jutting upward, remote and alone. Animals sought refuge from the sun, bunched in the sparse shade. In Laura's Dakota books, one of the landmarks is Lone Cottonwood, and now I understood the capital letters.

Beyond the 95th, shadow Indians on spectral buffalo hunts haunted the prairie. It seemed to me as though I had wandered here in my past life as a Dakota Sioux, in the days before grids, property lines and gas meters. In this life, I followed the buffalo, made camp and erected enormous tepees—then broke camp, roamed and set up again. In this life, I had no moving violations.

The vast, stark beauty of this new prairie silences Laura. The flowery grasses stretching endlessly before her under the dome of cloudless sky make her feel so strange that words escape her. Laura struggles to include Mary in what she sees, but literal description fails her. Turning to metaphor, Laura's gift for "making pictures when she talks" grows too woo woo for her pragmatic sister's tastes, who gets so cranky Laura gives up. No matter. To me, Laura's best moments are when she remains in her own thoughts, when she and Pa feel the same way without having to talk.

There was something else here that was not anywhere else. It was an enormous stillness that made you feel still. And when you were still, you could feel a great stillness coming closer.

Where Laura and Pa felt stillness, I felt enormous movement. Everything was movement, and the more I was still, the more everything moved around me. Winds churned the grasses so they circled like racecars around a motor speedway. I had learned to keep my hair braided or deal with an endless slapping of my face. The constant whooshing noise drove some pioneers insane, a condition described as "prairie madness," but to me the sound was a comfort, the way others enjoy rainfall or the sound of traffic.

In 1873, U.S. Senator Phineas W. Hitchcock of Nebraska took on the wind when he sponsored the Timber Culture Act, where settlers could file for second claim if they agreed to plant cottonwoods and fruit trees. Laurafans will remember the Ingalls family marveling how these great prairies would resemble Sherwood Forest one day. Didn't happen. Washington politicos were clueless as they dictated agricultural policy from white marble buildings thousands of miles away, and I had to admit, as I stood on this open land, I found myself glad they had been wrong.

The recent scheme has been to harness the wind as a renewable energy resource. Throughout western Minnesota, windmills appeared, and while their presence is controversial, personally I enjoyed the aesthetic. The giant, white pinwheels evoked the pyramids or statues of Easter Island, architecture that feels more alien than human made. With a pair of rose-colored glasses and a little squinting, they resembled three-pronged tepee poles reaching into the sky. I pulled over and watched for a while as the tines surged and stopped. They knew better than to fight the wind. A superior strategy is to ride the gust and let go.

Silver Lake marks a transitory section of Ingalls history, a period of neither-here-nor-there-ness. Pa works a temp job between farms. The Ingalls family is without a home, and they winter at the Surveyors' House, eating someone else's supplies. The Dakotas are neither civilized nor wild. Flocks of birds migrate overhead, wings flapping furiously on their way somewhere else. At the crux of this ambiguity is Laura's coming of age. She is no longer a girl, but not yet a woman.

At the railroad camp near Brookings, Laura meets her feisty doppelganger, Lena, a wild child with snappy eyes and curly black hair. With Lena, Laura experiences her final fling with childhood as they ride black ponies bareback across the open prairie, belting out songs about railroad men. Lena and Laura are a wild pair, "uncurbed."

One sunshiney morning Laura goes with Lena on her job to deliver the washing. They whoop *Hi Yi Yi, yi, yeee-ee!* and gallop across the plains until they are stopped by a muted, gray blot on the landscape. The laundress, a homesteader's wife, emerges from her shanty worn and dirty. Laura has never taken seriously Ma's repeated cautioning about how without her bonnet she'll turn brown as an Indian, but this woman is "brown as leather." The woman apologizes for her appearance and explains that she is behind in the chores since her girl, Lizzie, married and left home. Lizzie is thirteen. That's only a year older than Laura and Lena.

Pony high buzzkill.

The mother crows that marrying young is the way to go, but her scraggy appearance speaks to the contrary. Lena and Laura have always known that running a household would be their responsibility one day, but that day was only one day—until now.

Frontier House showed that for children and men, the pioneer life held great possibility for satisfaction. The men visibly puffed as they chopped wood and skinned animals. The children, once they crossed the whine barrier, grew lean and confident. By contrast, the women experienced a lot more house than frontier. You could see them erode under the strain of unrelenting and immutable chores. Three meals a day. Dishes. Laundry. The fire required constant tending, and stoking became a skill that required a certain obsessive quality—in the nineteenth century "slaving over a hot stove" was no hyperbole. Three meals a day. Dishes. Laundry.

"This is my existence right here. This is where I spend my days," said Kristen Brooks on *Frontier House*, motioning to her kitchen. "It's as though I've been transported to a labor camp," said Adrienne Clune, as the camera panned to a stumpy counter, one bowl of dingy water, and a few crumpled rags. In the final episode, Clune was reunited with her gleaming washer and dryer. The camera crew probably cut before she dry humped her appliances. Three meals a day. Dean. And Deluca.

Laura describes Ma's work in rosy terms, but we always knew she would rather be out helping Pa. In *Growing Up in the Country: Childhood on the Far Western Frontier*, historian Dr. Elliot West studied the journals of nineteenth-century pioneer children. He discovered that when they wrote about outdoor labor, "there seemed an intimate connection among the work, its setting, its results, and the children's sense of value and place," while "descriptions of the household tasks have little feel of excitement or pride in special achievement, little affection or involvement in the details around them." The outdoor chores were hard, but at least there was variety, fresh air and a chance at completion. In *Silver Lake*, Pa goes out every day until he shoots enough birds for a feather bed. Guess who plucks? The Ingalls family is without sons, so Laura is allowed to work outside, but one day, Laura knows she will have to trade the pitchfork and sunshine for the grimy rag in the corner. Lizzie's mother, ravaged by the grind, is the Ghost of Domestic Future pointing her skeletal, calloused finger to the washtub.

Laura's heart jerked, and then she seemed to feel it falling far, far down.

Laura's galloping days are coming to a close. The time has come to change from girl to young woman.

Over a hundred years later, I miserably botched this same transition.

I know I have described myself as a lonely, wimpy kid but even so, I mastered the basics with reasonable success. My brother wasn't born until I was seven, and until then, like Laura, I lived the life of a first-born son. I handed my father nails and crewed his sailboat. He took me camping. We played catch. Most Alabama girls minced around the playground, but I went to bat with confidence. "That's not a girl, that's Kelly!" the boys said, backing up and nodding at one another with respect. So far as school went (if we exclude "penmanship" and "keeping a notebook"), I was a good student. I managed the girly stuff, outfitting my Barbies in fashionable clothing and looking cute enough myself in one or two dresses. My Easy-Bake Oven cakes emerged, one after the other, perfectly risen and moist.

Once puberty hit, I didn't grow up so much as grow in, like a toenail.

My reckoning was a booklet. One day my mother opened the door, and instead of a Roald Dahl or Madeleine L'Engle book, she hurtled this gray missive before slamming the door. Spooked, I held the cover at arm's length—*Attaining Womanhood: A Doctor Talks to Girls About Sex*, by George W. Corner M.D. (implied subtitle: *There Will be Blood*). At first, I merely puzzled over the black doodles of Little Lulu morphing into June Cleaver, but the situation quickly turned horrific. Headless torsos and butchered body parts. Cross-sections of ovaries with grenade eggs spilling out. Fallopian tube nooses. My visceral reaction was immediate. *No way.* My mother acted as if she had pawned off a dead body, and I disposed of the corpse accordingly, burying the book beneath my days of the week panties and an equally disturbing eyelet-lace training bra. But there was no avoiding fate. The diagrams, the Fig. 6s and Fig. 7s, the charts and line drawings of pubic hair around a gaping maw kept resurfacing from the murky depths of my dresser. A floater.

Every time I saw the book my heart jerked, and I seemed to feel it falling far, far down.

Life is all bareback pony rides across the prairie until a girl gets her period.

I started when I was ten.

At the zoo.

Are you there, God? It's me, Kelly. Consider this our final conversation.

A box of tampons under the sink kills any illusion that a daughter can be a son. With puberty, a daughter's speed and strength will soon be eclipsed. Daughters grow boobs that flop when they run and must become careful how they sit. Daughters have to beware the wrong men or wind up in a life of misfortune, yet appeal to the right men or they have failed. Daughters have babies, which is either Life's Greatest Miracle or the Deserved Punishment of a Slut, depending.

At ten I was not equipped for these pressures. By twelve, I shot up to 5' 3" and by fourteen, I reached my adult height of 5' 9". I wanted to remain my Pa's Half-Pint, not get mistaken for his wife.

"Look at you, all big and grown-up!" my parents' friends would exclaim.

"Big" and "grown-up" were a one-two slug to my gut. When I heard other girls described as "little" or "darling," I crumpled, knowing I would never again be adorable. I was a behemoth. Like many girls who get too tall too soon, I hunched and tried walking with bent legs.

A son can be popular in junior high based on athletic prowess, money or talent, but a daughter, she has to be pretty. I tried. I woke up each morning to my arsenal: hair dryer, hot rollers, tweezers, eyelash curler, Maybelline Bloomin' Blues, Cover Girl Pro mascara, Kissing Sticks, eyebrow pencils, eyeliner, lip wax. Perched on the bathroom counter, I painstakingly mimicked the makeup charts from *Mademoiselle* and *Glamour*, assessing the shape of my face, carving cheekbones with powder, plotting how I would get out the door. If only I hadn't. School pictures are the cold, hard evidence of failure.

Sixth grade: Greasy hair yanked back by two barrettes, cayenne peppering of forehead acne, braces, tragic powder-blue terry cloth shirt.

Seventh grade: Perm on top of henna results in Orphan Annie catastrophe. Insistent wearing of new monogrammed sweater in ninety-degree heat causes line of too-dark orange foundation dripping down the neck.

Eighth grade: Feathered wings plastered with White Rain. Apricot blush applied like spackle. Brown frosted lipstick pinched from Mom gives me forty-year-old lips. Attempt to appear dramatic results in facial expression that makes subject resemble the victim of a bad taco.

Oh! My friends will say. *Surely, you didn't look that bad*, but if I show them, they turn quiet and change the subject. The tragedy is that these pictures aren't funny bad, like back issues of *Tiger Beat* magazine, but sad bad, like botched harelip surgery. When these photos were returned in homeroom, I held my breath, hoping to unveil a contact sheet of *Charlie's Angels*. Reality crushed. Who was this blotchy, defeated lumphead? Womanhood was a mystery to me as I sat alone for hours, locked in the bathroom with the Tampax diagram, trying to make sense of the situation. All I knew so far was that growing up was pretty miserable.

It was early evening when I saw the same Sign that once caused me to injure some roadside puckerbrush.

Laura Ingalls Wilder Homestead—De Smet, South Dakota.

I was back.

On the outskirts of town, I parked alongside a black and white notice tacked on a barbed wire fence that read, STABILIZATION POND SEWAGE CONTAMINATED WATER. This limp pool was all that remained of Silver Lake. A short wander down the road led to a gravel pit and cement mixer trucks. On my walk back, I saw two dumpsters overflowing with rusted metal and burnt wood next to a refuse pile of tires. I knew that the Surveyors' House had been moved into town. I wondered if the house had originally sat where the dumpsters were now.

This greeting was less than auspicious, but if I turned around, the Big Slough remained, even if it was a bit smaller. Silvery wormwood speckled the slopes where Laura and Carrie went sliding and saw the buffalo wolves. The marsh was a bright flash of green, brilliant to the eye after miles of dry prairie. The grasses rippled as gusts traveled across in waves. A unified frog chirp pulsed in the background, birdsong triplets claiming treble clef. The wind rushed in my ears. In Laura's day, the slough was so immense a person could become lost, but I could see a strip of yellow farmland across the way, bordered by a low ridge of cottonwoods. A railroad track ran in front. I practiced my Olympic balance beam routine on a rail, reviving a few moves from the summer I took gymnastics. It took a few times to cinch the gold.

February of 1880, Pa filed his claim, NE ¼ of 3-119-66. Within months, the town of De Smet sprung into place like a pop-up book. The day came when Pa went hunting at Silver Lake and found that settlers had driven all the wild birds away, but the Ingalls family wouldn't follow. Here they would stake their final claim. Going west was no longer the way to make progress. It was time to dig in, take a stand, establish roots, stop peeking over the horizon and stand firmly at the ground. Pa nails up the bracket, and Ma places the shepherdess.

The buffalo are gone, thought Laura. And now we're homesteaders.

The Books completely ignore menarche, yet another reason to love them. All the same, we know that Laura's girlhood is coming to a close, and that with adulthood comes adult responsibilities. For one, she has to earn her teaching certificate so the family can afford to send Mary to the College for the Blind. And Laura must face another challenge. Toward the end of *Silver Lake*, "those Wilder boys" ride by in a wagon drawn by Almanzo's brown Morgans, an omen sure as the Four Horsemen of the Apocalypse.

Once a therapist and I debated over whether I was depressed because of mental chemistry or because of circumstance.

"Well," he said, "stands to reason if you had a meaningful job and a steady relationship you might be happier."

Point taken. I was face planting at the big ones: work and love. There was a hole in the bucket. Chocolate Cake. Coconut Cake. I suspect that my childhood success was based on a lack of true challenges. Accustomed to easy A's and pats on the back, I never forged the core required to master true difficulties—a black hole makes for a lousy base of operations. The moment I was confronted with my first real challenge, puberty, I lost purchase and had struggled for footing ever since. Since moving to Montana, I had made changes, but if I wanted my new life to stick, I needed to connect the girl who swaggered at bat with the woman wobbling her way through life.

Flanked by a sewage pond on one side and a slough on the other, without a soul in sight, I had to say that the Dakota Boom was over. A pair of ducks glided low over the water; they knew better than to travel alone. I meditated on the whispering grasses and mentally rehearsed a few sound bites for my nightly call to My Manly, or, rather, my nightly recitation. I strived to entertain with my day's adventures, but at some point I became aware of my monologue sinking like a petrified bone in quicksand. *Cosmo* had cautioned me repeatedly that women are supposed to listen to men and act interested, but when I went quiet, My Manly didn't fill in the gaps. He didn't seem to like it when I asked questions either, and the conversation took on the flavor of a subject interrogation.

"Oh…," he would respond, his vowel plummeting into a dark well.

I knew exactly the expression, the one calling me to reach out, but you can't kiss someone and make it all better over the phone. I would hang up, suspecting I had failed somehow, followed by an urge to dial him right back up, even though I knew that was desperate. Desperate never works.

I sighed and jumped off the railroad track. It was time to stop playing Olympics. I appreciated my youthful spirit, but I needed to quit the kid games. I had spent my life running back for one last pony ride. Laura let the ponies go, knowing that she couldn't fly like a wild bird over Silver Lake forever.

Work and love.

It was time to face the big ones.

CHAPTER EIGHT
WITH A HANDFUL OF SALT AND A RIFLE

De Smet, South Dakota: *The Long Winter*

Mercy was a thing for gentler climes.
—Jack London

Every so often I would pull over and stare at the map, tracing and retracing my route. Not because I was lost. My direction, west, was straightforward enough. If in doubt, silos and grain elevators functioned as giant sundials. The point was that I enjoyed the time for repose. Maps relax me.

I sat in the car by the Big Slough and ran my finger over the thin black lines, chanting names softly to myself. Iroquois. Volga. Woonsocket. The syllables soothed. All this reliving of my angsty preteen past had me regressing to a similarly angsty state. This time I saw a town that gave me that *I know I've heard of this before but I don't know why* tug at my memory banks. Carthage, South Dakota, had nothing to do with the Books. What was it? I studied and obsessed and fidgeted until I extracted the factoid splinter—Carthage was the last place Chris McCandless worked before meeting his demise in the Alaskan woods. The story of this young man's self-imposed exile and subsequent starvation had been told by Jon Krakauer in his best-selling book, *Into the Wild*, followed by the movie directed by Sean Penn.

Into the Wild is another book I have read so many times it could be said I once lived there. I have always felt a certain kinship with Chris McCandless. We both grew up soft in the South, admiring Jack London's tales of Arctic survival. Mired in suburban ennui, we thrilled over the transformation of Buck in *The Call of the Wild* from pampered pooch to dominant primordial beast. I suspect the complicated, often contradictory codes of southern behavior confused Chris, just as they perplexed me. By contrast, the black-and-white world of London's Alaska presented refreshingly clear directives. *Eat or be eaten. Kill or be killed. The law of the club and fang.*

Around July in Alabama, the prospect of freezing to death struck me as a dream come true. During the summers of my deep southern childhood, dogs asphyxiated, grandparents collapsed and treks across the Piggly Wiggly blacktop were an exercise in misery. The very words Errand Day imbued me with dread. These afternoons, I suffocated in the back of our two-door Celica while Mom worked through her endless lists. The black leather seats seared my pink thighs as I tugged at my shorts, skin melting on muscle like broiled cheese. To this day, I remain convinced that the state of Alabama conspired to dehydrate its children in a plot to create astronaut food for the Huntsville Space Center. At schools, playgrounds, summer camps and church youth groups, adults rationed our furtive gulps of water before rushing us along to the next hot, dusty activity.

Tales of desert survival held little appeal. To escape shrieking cicadas, melted popsicles and our humpy toy poodle, I turned to shrieking blizzards, ice floes and husky sled dogs. There was Jack London, but also *Julie of the Wolves, Alive* and *Endurance: Shackleton's Incredible Voyage.* Reigning supreme was *The Long Winter,* the story of the Ingalls family surviving seven months of winter storms on the prairie. I could barely wrap my Southland brain around the isolated, stark frontier of the Dakota Territory, an unspeakably exotic locale. De Smet might have been the Himalayas or ice planet Hoth for all I knew of it. My childhood fears over Laura's ordeal so seriously scarred me, I almost didn't move to Montana, terrified at the idea of living somewhere people kept an axe and a blanket in the trunk "just in case." Turns out I survived just fine with a warm-blooded boyfriend and a jacket like a sleeping bag. Winters were a shock, but manageable with ready access to Applewood smoked bacon and espresso.

On my trip, I would not experience a Great Plains winter, much less how Laura lived through one without central heat or reliable supplies. This was a serious gap in my journey, but maybe there was a way to make do. I looked back down at the map. Carthage was forty-five miles south and west. I cranked the engine and found myself headed in that direction.

The Ingalls family did not come to the Dakotas in search of wilderness adventure. They wanted a farm. But while the railroads were quick to advertise the rich, virgin sod, they were loath to report prairie fires, tornadoes, drought, locust plagues and long winters. Settlers, in the hurry to claim free land, didn't stop to assess long-range forecasts. All persons with Dakota winter experience (i.e., the Sioux) had been killed or evicted. In naïveté the settlers arrived expecting a normal winter, the sort that kills bugs and provides a chance to gather 'round the hearth, knit scarves and pop popcorn. Then the blizzards hit, and even immigrants from Scandinavia and Russia experienced a shock.

On the Great Plains, blizzards roar unchecked across the open fields, and temperatures reach 40 below on a regular basis. Before reliable forecasts and sleeping bag jackets, the cold was more than miserable. The isolation of the settlers made going for help or supplies nearly impossible. Before, I surmised that living 160 acres apart from the closest neighbor would be lonely. Winter made this distance deadly. The Ingalls were fortunate in that they had a place in town, but even that didn't guarantee safety. Dakota blizzards had such blinding white winds it was common to stray a few feet and freeze to death.

Sometimes Laura (as she put it) "stretched a point" for the sake of drama, but this winter, named the Snow Winter of 1880–81, is recorded, meteorological fact. The trial began October 15 with a three-day snowstorm that took out the entire Upper Midwest. After that, a series of nonstop blizzards pummeled the area for seven months, just as the Sioux in Harthorn's store predicted. The last train to make Huron arrived on January 4, and the trains didn't get through again until May. David Laskin, in *The Children's Blizzard*, which recounts a specific, disastrous blizzard of 1888, notes that *Long Winter* is an accurate account of the typical Plains settler experience that year— twisting hay for fuel, near starvation, train vigils and the constant grinding of seed wheat in a coffee grinder to bake bread.

The year 1880 was the peak of the Dakota Boom. Many families, such as the Ingalls family, were new arrivals. These hastily erected homesteads were not the established farms Laura describes in *Big Woods* with supplies of nuts, dried fruit, barrels of cornmeal and cured meats. Less than a year is barely enough time for a turnip crop, especially if the ground is going to freeze in October. When the first blizzard hit so early, many had not yet dug out their potatoes, milled their grain, or purchased the necessary supplies. Pa was right to be in a hurry to unearth his crop, albeit meager in number and size—those potatoes would be rationed over the next months, and potatoes were more than many settlers had.

The premise of *Frontier House* was to see if in six months modern families could prove up their homesteads enough to survive winter, thereby presenting the same challenge nineteenth-century pioneers faced. By show's end, the Frontier Valley families accomplished a great deal. They built homes, dug root cellars, planted crops, baked bread from scratch and raised livestock. The ragtag cast of twenty-first-century greenhorns morphed into plucky homesteaders.

For the show's finale, historical experts came out to inspect the homesteads and pass sentence. The last few weeks the families busted out their best pioneer moves, hoping for a good report card, the two competitive families pulling out all the stops. Judgment Day everyone stood anxious and expectant. The experts barely glanced at the thriving vegetable gardens or the livestock pens. They marched straight to the feeble stacks of chopped wood and shook their heads, their verdict swift and sure—no two out of three making it here. Everyone would have frozen to death.

The families sulked for a moment, shrugged and headed back to their insulated houses and central heat. They knew from the onset that they would only homestead in Montana summer through early fall—vacation season.

Long Winter, like any worthwhile survival story, includes a meticulous tally of the family's winter supplies. We all love to catalog food. After trick-or-treating each Halloween, my chief pleasure came from the sorting afterward. I had categories according to type: chocolate bars, tart candies, chewy candies and weird candies. Next, I divided my loot into subcategories (Smarties versus SweeTarts), and last, I ranked in order of preference (Three Musketeers: Number One). Food brings out the weird in all of us. Of all my lessons learned waiting tables, this is the one I will never forget. I witnessed family lineages dissolve over breakfast buffets and couples divorce over crab cakes. That people melted down on a regular basis over baskets of chips and salsa in our land of plenty once mystified me, but I came to understand that food is such an elemental need, it reduces people to their basest nature.

Jon Krakauer points out that Chris McCandless was a great reader of Russian novels and a philosopher, yet the closer he came to death, his big books and big ideas held little solace. His Alaskan journal entries pared down to terse meal recitations: Duck. Squirrel. Porcupine. Ptarmigin. Berries. Gray bird. Another squirrel. Another porcupine. More berries. MOOSE!

Chris went to Alaska so he could delve into the inner workings of the soul. His discovery:

The Great Holiness of Food, *the Vital Heat.*

Once, My Manly took me to the Barclay II Supper Club in Anaconda, Montana. Stepping inside the cinderblock walls created a time warp, as though John Wayne must be somewhere sawing at a rare porterhouse. Black leather booths cradled red wax candles and baskets of Captain's Wafers. A dusty brandy snifter on the vacant piano patiently awaited the return of MacArthur. For weeks afterward, I regaled fellow starving artists with the tale of my meal: Shrimp cocktail. Salad. Relish tray of celery and carrots. Salami. Cheese. Baked potato. Texas toast. Side of spaghetti and ravioli. Ice cream sundae. STEAK.

Polish all that off with a coupla Jack and Cokes served on a silver tray by a bartender in a bow tie, and if that doesn't make your woman say "I love you," then I can't help you. I wrote the details of our meal on a cocktail napkin and stashed it in the Valentine candy box.

I arrived in Carthage as the sun went down and toured the grid. It didn't take long to locate the Cabaret, the town bar. While Chris had worked at the grain elevator here, he had struck up a friendship with his boss, and this was where they had hung out. Chris was an accomplished entertainer and would play the piano and sing for the crowd.

I pulled over and turned off the engine. It was dark, and the streets were quiet. The question was, now what? I knew that bellying up at the watering hole was de rigueur for the adventurous traveler. Wasn't I supposed to go and swig hooch with the locals? I checked my driver's license. Yep, twenty-one. But if a gift shop made me nervous, walking alone into a bar in a prairie dress took social anxiety to a whole new level. I rapped my fingernails on the steering wheel and reviewed the possibilities:

(1) Go in and have a drink.

(2) Drive back to De Smet.

I performed a mental test run of option one.

I swagger in and find an empty stool at the bar. A woman with cropped brunette hair dressed in a frayed gingham shirt leans over and lifts an eyebrow.

"Bourbon, neat," I say.

"Where you from?" The bartender squints as she free pours in a jelly jar.

"De Smet. Heard y'all are big stars now, what with the movie coming out. Hanging out with Sean Penn and the like."

"Oh yeah. We're rolling out a red carpet at the Prairie Inn. Carthage is gonna be a real tourist hot spot."

"It'll probably bring more business than the stinking hog confinement," says a man.

"All those smelly hogs do nothing but scare off people who use the lake," grumbles another.

"Sean Penn and hogs belong together. They both smell. Ha ha," says the bartender. For that, I buy her a shot. We clink glasses and toss back.

From the pool table a young man approaches, doing that sway, shuffle and glance-around move men do when they want to talk to you but are feeling shy. He's lean and rangy, like a mule colt.

We exchange hellos.

"So are you like, uh, Amish?" He cocks his head to one side. His tanned forehead has the wrinkled crease of a man much older.

"No, I'm Laura Ingalls."

"Your dress is cool," he nods.

"Hey, Eddie," barks the bartender. "Maybe you should try and work show business. You can sure act when you're trying to pick up women. Ha ha."

With that I snapped to in the Camry. De Smet, it was. No way was I going in. First off, there was the issue of Ma Ingalls blowing a gasket from the grave, but even if I didn't drink, even if I just popped in for a look-see, the situation was a whole lot more complicated for me than Jon Krakauer. That's because a man alone at a bar is a man alone at a bar, but a woman alone at a bar is woman looking for a man.

I settled for a drive-by of the grain elevator instead, cursing the Tampax diagram once more.

At the heart of every arctic survival story is the principle that the deserving live while the rest are handed Darwin Awards. Jack London didn't invent this concept, but he did immortalize it in *The Call of the Wild* with John Thornton, Buck's third owner, but only *master*. John Thornton is the Arctic Man. London describes in terse, testosterone prose how Thornton trekked fearlessly into the wild, needing only a "handful of salt and a rifle" to sustain himself. We all want to believe that if thrust in a survival situation, our characters would prove kind yet unsentimental, smart but instinctual, fearless yet respectful of the savage elements, and that we could, if necessary, tame a wolf. Most of us prefer to believe these truths from the comfort of our La-Z-boy recliners. Not McCandless. Weary of suburban comforts and the empty material life, he sought a test, a way to come of age. He wanted something worth crying about, so he grabbed a bag of rice and a rifle and struck out.

The once soft southerner almost made the grade. Krakauer details the twists and turns that could have altered fate. He makes a good case that Chris, while foolhardy by Alaskan standards, was in many ways wily and resourceful. He found shelter, gathered edible plants and hunted game before making his tragic mistake with a moose (MOOSE!). His bullet hit the mark, but then he smoked the meat (as instructed by South Dakotan hunters) instead of air-drying it (as he would have been instructed by Alaskan hunters, had he thought to ask). If he had read London closely, he would have noted that John Thornton brought a handful of salt, not a bag of rice, although before we get too critical, it bears mentioning that London was no John Thornton either. (And really? Was a handful enough?) The author only spent a few weeks in Alaska before beating a retreat to sunny California where he died a corpulent alcoholic.

The Ingalls family, despite their resourcefulness, also nearly fell victim to starvation due to underestimating the severity of an unknown land. Two-thirds into *Long Winter*, the rationing of supplies begins in earnest. Pa and Laura look on worriedly as Ma pours the last of the wheat into the coffee grinder. Laura must be strong for Carrie and sing the song of Canaan as the family endures yet another raging blizzard, but inside, she's counting wheat kernels.

Enter our hero.

Almanzo Wilder (future love interest) enlists Cap Garland (hottie) on a daring quest for wheat. There is a break in the storms, and although another blizzard could hit at any moment, the young men strike out on the frozen prairie. On this venture Almanzo proves himself to be a John Thornton of the highest degree, making the right decision time and again under stressful conditions. The adventurers find the homesteader and finesse the transaction. A blizzard on their heels, Cap and Almanzo arrive in town with their haul, saving the town from starvation.

Parade!

Or was Almanzo just a luckier Chris McCandless? One blizzard at the wrong moment and he would have been done for. There was no absolute need for Almanzo to put his life in jeopardy, never mind Cap's. Almanzo had seed wheat stashed behind a false wall. He even wound up offering the homesteader more than the going rate for wheat. Monetarily speaking, Almanzo might have come out ahead selling his seed wheat over planting a crop.

Almanzo's defense was that he didn't move across the country to be a coward. He had hauled the wheat raised and threshed by his own hand a great distance. Probably this wheat was of a higher quality than what could be purchased at the store, but I suspect there was more at stake. Almanzo—like Chris—needed to define his coming of age. Perhaps it's better to risk than swat at the miasma of depression. Chris has been criticized for his adventures, but it could be argued how he lived and died was better than a life of quiet desperation. For much of my life fear of change, fear of consequences, had kept me stuck. And I had spent much of my life fending off the mental black cloud.

The choice: risk and come of age, or wander in circles.

A shiver racked my body. In the Dakotas, winter is never far away. Even the July night air sliced like a straight razor. Somehow, nineteenth-century pioneers weathered blizzards in claim shanties with nothing but a sack of wheat and dried hay. Come January, this land would be a glittering white expanse in all directions, but I wouldn't be here to see it.

I turned up the heat and drove back to De Smet.

CHAPTER NINE
IN WHICH WORK IS WORKED OUT

De Smet, South Dakota: *Little Town on the Prairie*

I padded in like a teenager sneaking in past curfew. The Prairie House Manor Bed and Breakfast was nestled amongst the small neighborhood of old houses around the De Smet downtown. There was a homey, lived-in touch to the place—marshmallow sofas, board games, magazines and patchwork pillows. A Ma was taking care of the house. You could feel it. I glanced over the book collection and scanned for the Little House books. They were there, only the blue-covered edition. Check-in consisted of an unlocked door with the room key taped on the front. Try that in Los Angeles.

My room was upstairs. I spread out, luxuriating in the financial benefit of the Prairieland vacation—$69 per night for two twin daybeds and a full, roomy bath in a beautiful house with an enclosed front porch. I would be here a few days so I had the chance to settle in. On the opposite bed I placed the Books, my camera and journal, and a minute after that, my blue dress. I slipped on a worn tank and swiped pair of My Manly's boxer shorts. Once in bed, I curled up in the pink and country-blue double wedding ring quilt. A hailstorm hit as I pulled up the covers. Stones pelted the HVAC unit outside, creating a thunderous racket, but I was safe inside.

In *Long Winter*, Laura fights the elements, but this interlude only staves off the inevitable. Beginning with *Little Town*, Laura has to return and face the murkier battles of adolescence. What will be her vocation? Who will be her friends? Who will she date? With trademark Laura spirit, she tackles these challenges one by one. This was the exact point in my life I began to flop around like a salmon working its way up the wrong river. For the redux, I would employ a more organized approach. Instead of addressing everything that had gone wrong in my life at once (Wah!), I would break the situation down. Laura had the sense to tackle her job situation first before taking on a relationship. I would follow her lead.

When I was a teenager, my responsibility was to get good grades so I could go to college. Once in college, I was to continue to get good grades so I could get a real job. I dutifully traveled the red-bricked paths of the University of North Carolina, going from class to class, ticking requirements off my list. At the time, the situation suited me fine. I enjoyed classes and delved happily into subjects ranging from the geology of North America to Ptoon kouros. Not that I had any idea what I would do with this information after college. I understood a "real job," was the desired result, but I didn't know what a "real job" was (except that it offered health insurance and a retirement plan), or who would give me said "real job."

Predictably, haplessness begat haplessness. Upon graduation, I did not become a doctor and take my parents to Italy. Instead, I embarked upon a new circular route from the table, to the bar, to the kitchen, to the table. Much to my parents' chagrin and my own, I became a career waiter.

I woke up the following morning lazy. Not wanting to get out of bed, I overslept and missed breakfast. Then I was hungry and feeling sorry for myself, and the more I felt sorry for myself, the less I wanted to get up. Lying in bed suffering the existential funk pretty much described my four years of college. And the sixteen years after that. I was slipping back into the worn grooves of neurotic thought patterns, wondering why I was here, questioning myself. How, exactly, was a tour of pioneer gift shops in the rural Midwest supposed to change my life? Like the leftover morning coffee I found downstairs, I was old and bitter. Then I re-remembered: my ways of thinking weren't to be trusted. That's why I was putting my faith in Laura. I released the mental struggle and allowed routine to take over. Time to suit up.

The suck of breath.

The zip.

Apron.

Bonnet.

Camera.

Wallet.

Books.

Rouge Bingo lipstick.

There are two distinct tourist centers in De Smet. One is run by the Laura Ingalls Wilder Memorial Society, a nonprofit organization "dedicated to the preservation of the Ingalls and Wilder heritages." The other is a privately owned, pioneer version of Colonial Williamsburg called "Ingalls Homestead," situated on a section of the old claim, out on "Laura's living prairie." There is yet a third group, the Laura Ingalls Wilder Pageant Society, in charge of De Smet's annual production (similar to the pageant at Walnut Grove), which I would attend later.

The Laura Ingalls Wilder Memorial Society Information Center was only a few blocks away, so I walked. From all the driving, my legs were in danger of locking into permanent right angles, and a morning in the fetal position hadn't helped. I lurched down the quiet neighborhood of little houses and trees until I found the headquarters, a Victorian white house with stacked siding and a small porch. The usual suspects milled around out front (families and retirees, plus one tall, auburn-haired woman in a bright blue dress). De Smet seemed to have a steadier stream of visitors than the other homesites. Located about an hour and a half from I-90, the stop can be worked in on the way to the Black Hills, Deadwood, Mt. Rushmore or Yellowstone. I suspected some tourists were also pageant pregamers such as myself.

I skipped the shopping and got down to business. A young woman with a milk-toothed smile sold me a ticket for the tour. We stood nose to nose in dueling prairie garb, hers a fawn-colored calico.

"One, please," I said.

"This ticket covers the Surveyors' House and the house Ma and Pa lived in. The next tour leaves in forty minutes."

"You mean the building Pa had in town?" I said.

"Nooooo. That building no longer stands." The cashier paused and gave me a moment to absorb this information. I suppose my attire broadcasted *fragile freaky Laurafan: handle with care*. She adopted a sympathetic expression, squishing up her plump cheeks until her expression began to resemble one of those granny dolls made of panty hose. She started again, this time in a low, soothing tone.

"The house on Third Street is where the Ingalls family lived after they sold the homestead. After Laura married and moved in with Almanzo."

"I don't remember a house on Third Street," I said.

"Nooooo. Laura didn't write about it. But you can see Mary's beadwork," she chirped, thinking this informational tidbit would cheer me up. "The cabinets Pa built are still there, as well as many other Ingalls artifacts."

"Ma and Pa sold the homestead," I intoned.

"In 18—wait. Was it 1882?" she said.

"Excuse me," I said.

I trudged back to the Prairie Manor, stomped up the stairs and crawled back in bed, pulling the quilt over my boots, skirts and head.

I knew this section of the trip might get rough as I confronted some of the tetchier areas of my past. Complicating the issue was that I didn't, truth be told, care to know too much about the "real" Ingalls family, nervous I might learn something unsavory. Dr. Holtz had already planted some unpleasant stories about Rose and Laura that were rattling inside my brain. The time was coming when I would have to warp beyond adolescence into the big mess of fact versus fiction, and what happens when we learn the truth about our idols. I had been indulging myself in baby steps when it was time to ride the zip line across the canyon. I couldn't control what information might come my way as I transitioned from Laura the little girl into Laura the adult. *Ma and Pa had sold the homestead.* I confess that my undying belief had been that Ma and Pa lived their entire lives on those 160 acres, proving up the land until it ran like a Japanese auto plant.

This was grown-up-ness in all its hairy, uncensored glory.

My grand scheme of staying in bed until the universe collapsed wasn't going very well. Problem One: I had downed an entire carafe of coffee on an empty stomach—I was hopelessly awake. Problem Two: Guilt set in pretty much the second I lifted the quilt over my eyes. That's the downside of traveling with Laura. She's great company and you never tire of her, but there's a high standard at work. Hiding out made me feel like a lame-o. Adrenaline and guilt, I discovered, make poor bed partners. I threw aside the quilts and pulled myself up by the Frye bootstraps. By the time I walked back to the information center, I was just in time for the departing tour gathering on the front steps.

The guide appeared as if from behind a velvet curtain, and the group fell silent. Her prairie dress was dark and plain, a selection from Jonathan Edwards couture, her silver hair twisted in a tight bun. She pulled back her lips in a faint smile so that we would know to shush. A product of two teachers, I know this look, and I know to obey it. Stat. When she spoke, she raised her chin and eyebrows as if to lecture over the tops of our heads. Even though she was shorter than me, I felt as though I needed to stand on tippy-toe to hear. Then she turned on her heels and took off at a clip. We tourists bumbled behind, our limbs and minds sluggish from miles of travel, clutching our tickets like waifs in a Russian bread line.

The Surveyors' House stood apart from the other cute white houses because of its flat lumber siding. And, may I say, it was adorable. Word was that the Surveyors' House might seem disappointing, for while described by Laura as "big," the house would look small by modern standards, but I wasn't let down in the least. To me the house looked perfect, exactly the marvel Laura had described.

We crowded in the main room with glossy white walls and glossy gray floors. If the exterior was spot on, the interior made me uncomfortable, the sanitarium white a bit oppressive, needing a scuff or two to look lived in. The room was sparsely furnished with an organ, a stove and a table with a red and white checkerboard cloth doing its best to add some cheer to the situation.

"The Surveyors' House, dating back to 1879, is the oldest building in De Smet. It was moved in 1885 from its original site on Silver Lake to where it stands now. The Ingalls wintered over here in 1880 for five months when they first arrived. The house was purchased by the Memorial Society in 1967 and has been open for visitors since 1968. Over twenty-five thousand people a year..."

And, um, from there I tuned out a bit. My excuse was that two women whispering in the back distracted me. I suppose I'm old-school enough to believe people should appear attentive even if they are secretly pondering lunch. The situation made me indignant, and now that I was all huffy, I was really having trouble concentrating.

For distraction, I discreetly peered into the pantry to my left, which held little jars and barrels to simulate provisions. The pantry was cordoned off, which was frustrating. I understood that people couldn't tear willy-nilly through a historical landmark, but the coolest, the absolute coolest part of the Surveyors' House chapter is when Ma and Pa let Laura run ahead so she can explore on her own. Laura runs her fingers over the canned goods and opens every barrel so she can inspect the corn meal, flour and big slabs of salted fish. The adult me knew that it was impractical to stock real corn meal and salt pork so tourists could rummage around, but the kid me went pouty. My hands yearned for touch.

The guide knew the teacher trick of dynamics for silencing gossipers and waking up space cadets.

"IN THIS CORNER you can see a whatnot, built just as Laura describes in *By the Shores of Silver Lake*. This room, that Laura described as 'large,' is actually only 12 by 15 feet, 4 inches..."

I snapped to, but the misbehavers continued their mutterings. At that, the guide stopped midsentence. The room hushed except for the two women, who then realized everyone had turned to stare. Their jaws froze midflap. The guide directed her thin smile toward them.

"Excuse me, if you have something you need to discuss I'd appreciate it if you did so somewhere else."

Vacation, we had just learned, does not excuse poor manners.

The women flushed red. The guide finished her lecture, but I was too mortified to even try and listen anymore. At the conclusion of the talk, we were told we had time to look around, but as the other rooms were forbidden, there wasn't much to investigate. The upstairs was off limits, and this situation was even worse than the pantry because I couldn't see. I leaned over the velvet ropes and craned my neck as far as I dared, feeling like a schoolboy sneaking looks up a skirt. I debated breaking in later that night—I didn't imagine De Smet security was all that high—and just as quickly dismissed the notion. Once a fan crosses the creeper line there's no going back.

We skulked around, speaking in hushed whispers, trying not to point.

Is that the real organ? The one that Mary played?

I don't know.

What about that stove? Did Ma cook on that stove?

I don't know.

I wonder what the upstairs looks like.

We were all afraid the guide had covered these topics while we weren't paying attention, and now none of us were brave enough to ask. After our muted, sober explorings, we were informed we would split up and meet again at the Ingalls residence on Third Street. Once outside everyone scattered for their cars. The distance was far enough that it would take fifteen minutes to hoof it, and I stood there, stymied, not knowing what to do. The Camry was back at Prairie House Manor.

I strolled over to the guide and gave her my best winsome look. I needed a ride, but I was also hoping for a schmooze, a little inside chat, some LIW one-on-one girl talk. I certainly had not been talking while she was talking, and I liked to think she appreciated my good behavior. Once more, I suppose, I hoped to be recognized as a special Laurafan, distinct from the commonplace tourist.

"Oh, I walked here," I said. "I didn't know we'd have to drive."

In Alabama, this broad of a hint would be the equivalent of sticking my hitchhiker's thumb up your grits, but this was the Midwest, so I pressed my point a bit further.

"Do you think I can walk and make it in time for the talk?"

The guide didn't break stride.

"You had better walk fast then!" she called over her shoulder before getting in her sedan and shutting the door.

I know hitchhiking is generally considered the pursuit of seedy lowlifes, and maybe my dress made me look like some kind of kook, but as one grown woman in a full-length skirt to another, I had hoped for kinship. I had to admit, the Midwestern Victorian Beefeater brigade was getting me down. I decided I would show Ms. Mighty Memorial Society by running the entire way. She'd be sorry as I heaved for oxygen during her next round of pontifications. With prodding I could probably work up an asthma wheeze, maybe even a full-blown attack. My grand revenge scheme was shaping up nicely until I realized if I didn't catch a ride I would miss the whole shebang.

Across the street I spied two young women, a purple tie-dyed version of Abbot and Costello. Their wagon was covered in peace sign and rainbow stickers. A quick profiling assessment told me I had found my ride.

"Hey! I don't have my car. Can I jump in?" Forget the sashay and southern charm. It was time to get my Yankee on. After all, just like Laura, my father was from New York State.

"Sweet threads." The rounder of the two in a "Save the Frickin' Narwhales" t-shirt motioned to my dress.

"I'm not sure there's room in the back..." The lean one, and apparent owner of the vehicle, peered with a doubtful expression at the back of their car.

"No problem!" I flipped back the seat and inserted myself among the backpacks, Mexican blankets and half-eaten chip bags. I launched a barrage of words—when in doubt, talk them to death. We established that I was not Amish, just odd, and that they were juniors in college on the Crazy Jack Kerouac Totally Far Out Summer Road Trip. I described how I was snubbed by the elder stateswoman of the Memorial Society, from the kiss-off wave to the slam of the car door.

"Can you believe that?" I said. "I mean, I know I'm in this dress and all, but it's pretty obvious I'm not crazy."

"The house is just a few blocks up, right?" said Cranky.

"That old gal's a trip. She burned those ladies in the back. I was like, daaaaang," said Plumpie Rainbow as she offered me a toke off her one-hitter. Plumpie was the one who had seen the Sign on I-90 and insisted they veer off.

"Laura freakin' Ingalls," said Plumpie. She reached for the Cool Ranch Doritos. "That was some crazy shit. It was like an omen."

"Like a Sign," I offered. "You know, not a road sign but a *Sign*."

"That's right. That's it. A Sign. You are so wise. So wise."

"Ooo, Cheetos," I said, pulling a bag from the floor.

"Go for it," said Plumpie.

"Here we are!" said Cranky, parking with a sudden jerk of the gear shift.

We had landed right in front of my Camry. It turned out that the Ingalls house was two doors down from the Prairie Manor. I gave Mr. Turtle a little wave, brushed the orange crumbs from my apron and wiped my mouth, a bit bummed the ride was so short. I hadn't connected with a Laurafan like that since the Amish man in Kansas. I could tell Plumpie and I were on the verge of a huge Laura geek out.

Most of the group had already reconvened outside. Plumpie, Cranky and I slipped in the back. The guide stood at the front door, to the right of a KEEP OFF THE GRASS sign. I knew now what it was about her smile. It reminded me of the disastrous term Miss Wilder taught school, and the time she said "birds in their little nests agree" while the class squirmed. No wonder I was nervous. As Laura pointed out, birds in their little nests do everything but agree, and usually shove the smallest one out. The guide's face began to swell and seemed more and more to me like the suspended head of the Wizard of Oz. The grass turned a vibrant shade of chlorophyll, almost fluorescent. The green was calling me, and I had a terrible urge to stomp all over Emerald City lawn. The more I stared at the grass, the more it glowed this beautiful, bright, mossy, deep sea green, green… green… I reached my toe out. *I'll just touch the edge. Which is not really walking on the grass.*

"Yo," I felt a jab in my arm. It was Plumpie, poking me. The group had moved on, leaving me alone, gaping at the lawn.

Inside we huddled in the living room behind the velvet rope.

"The Ingalls family lived in this house from 1887 to 1928…"

I tried not to look at the portraits of Charles and Caroline Ingalls, their austere pioneer expressions staring down at me. I couldn't quite reconcile the twinkly-eyed Pa and gentle Ma with these grim reapers. I concentrated on the wallpaper, which I learned had taken some doing to reconstruct. It was a huge print, probably too bold for the size of the room, but festive in its vibrant, yellow way. The Third Street house had real furniture and rugs. Compared to the log cabins of Pepin or Independence, it was the Biltmore Estate.

Although disappointed that Pa and Ma didn't live forever on the homestead, I consoled myself that at least they really did live 'til death did them part. Pa and Ma divorcing would have been the end of me. I could see where moving back to town was understandable in older age. In the kitchen we saw the cupboards Pa had built for Ma. I wondered what it would be like to cook in a kitchen knowing that My Manly had customized it especially for me. Handcrafted cabinetry struck me as romantic, personal.

Mary's room was off to the side, her spinster twin bed against the wall. This made me a little sad, but not shocked. Mary had been on the nun track from day one. I wondered how Mary transitioned back home after her studies at the College for the Blind in Vinton. The Books focus on the challenge of sending Mary to college. But then what? She was probably frustrated over the uselessness of her degree, and as a woman with a Bachelor's in English literature and philosophy, I knew exactly how Mary must have felt.

We couldn't go up the real stairs (too fragile), so we went around back where metal stairs had been attached like a fire escape, trekking up single file. Two of the rooms were furnished with Rose's belongings from her adult life, although Rose had only spent her early childhood here. Rose's writing desk was there, large, wooden and broad with an Underwood typewriter. Her office looked like the Ideal Romantic Writer's Life, as if just by sitting there you'd begin madly clickety-clacking (ping!) the sequel to *War and Peace*.

I once watched a documentary that featured the Shroud of Turin. For the privilege of a sighting, people pilgrimage to Italy and wait hours upon hours in line. When their time comes, they are ushered in a crowded room, allowed a few minutes and then guided out, so the next group can be waved through. This tour was a little like that. Before I knew it, I found myself back out on Third Street.

Plumpie and Cranky drove off in search of Jerry Garcia's ghost (ultimate destination: Haight-Ashbury). I stood alone on the

sidewalk, watching the wagon putter and turn the corner. A weight
sunk in my chest. Sometimes you don't realize how lonely you are
until you've been with people again, and then they leave.

I wandered downtown in search of company. Main Street remained
a collection of local businesses, although commerce looked sporadic.
Paved roads and concrete sidewalks had replaced the dirt and
wooden boardwalks. There was a coffee shop in lieu of the Wilder
Feed Store, and the local saloon was tucked away in a cinderblock
building (like many small-town Midwestern bars) on a side street.
The Laura draw hadn't brought about a Ye Olde Downtowne of
tourist attractions, although a version of the Loftus Store remained.
Some buildings looked vintage while others appeared to be of newer
construction. The overall effect was that the downtown hadn't quite
decided what it wanted to be when it grew up, and in that way, it
hadn't changed a bit since 1880.

The Timber Culture Act failed, but like many western towns,
De Smet had managed to cultivate a few tree-lined streets. The
canopy oppressed after my days on the prairie; branches loomed
overhead like giant birds of prey. Coming downtown had been a
mistake. I wanted out, back in the open, somewhere I could clear
my head. Everything was picking up speed. Baby Grace was suddenly
an overweight, married lady nicknamed "Auntie Fat." Carrie had
fallen victim to diabetes in Keystone. The dour portraits, Mary's
spinster bed, my loneliness, the fear of disappointment, a realization
that for the past week I had engaged in more involved conversations
with a stuffed turtle than my actual boyfriend—thoughts in all these
directions gave me a panicky feeling.

I took off for the open space. Within minutes I was past the tree
barrier. Back in the unfenced prairie, the nervous grip of
claustrophobia eased from my chest.

Standing on a Dakota prairie is the closest a person can get to
walking on water. Perhaps that's because sixty-five million years ago
the Great Plains was the Cretaceous Sea. Today the prairie is the
reflective image of that ancient water, two sides of the same world.
Cloud shadows raced across the rippling surface. The grasses tossed

and turned. My skirts fluttered like a kite, as though if I jumped precisely the right way, I could launch.

I chose the earth. I flopped and rolled like a horse, just as Laura does at the end of *Silver Lake*, her last gasp at youthful play. I spread my arms and legs and absorbed the huge sky, soaking up the dry air and sun. The world should always be July in South Dakota. Lying belly down on the ground, I pulled out my copy of *Silver Lake* and reread the part where Laura runs ahead to see the Surveyors' House. What if the magic had dulled? By dissecting the Books with an adult mind, I might lose the childhood thrill, but soon as my hand turned the page, it became six years old again, smooth and pink. I relived Laura's thrill over the Surveyors' House stocked pantry. What was it about those oyster crackers? I read through to the end where the Ingalls family moves to the claim shanty, where even if Ma and Pa didn't stay forever, they lived for a very long time.

Occasionally a car drove by, the motoring sound a reminder of the present. I wondered what they saw, this bright blue-flowered blight on the dried yellow grass. Once in a while someone slowed down, but no one, no one, ever stopped.

Little Town opens with Laura's first paid work outside the home, a temp job sewing buttonholes for Mr. Clancy. The illustration of Laura walking to work that first morning with Pa, father and daughter so serious as they stride holding hands, has always had a deep impression on me. The time has come for Laura to be judged for her work ethic outside of the home. If she could not hold down a job, she would not be able to help send Mary to college, and she would let down her family.

My first job was washing dishes in a university cafeteria for $4 an hour. The meal plan was based on all you can eat, but as the food was of questionable origin, students didn't eat so much as craft sculptures. The worst assignment was pulling flatware off the plastic trays as they moved down what was called "the gravy train." I emptied glasses packed with wet napkins and rifled through the remains in search of forks and knives. After work, despite the plastic gloves and the scrubbing with lemon juice, my hands smelled of masticated Alpo. But the scant checks kept me out of debt and even paid for a few trips out of town.

That summer I worked at Shoney's, my first real job waiting tables. Tips were lean. I remember the time one of my coworkers received five dollars on Shrimp Night, a full 15 percent on the tab. The entire waitstaff gathered around the bill and gawked for a solid minute. Every night I staggered out to my car, my apron a weight belt of change. At home I poured my lucre on the bed and sorted my coins into piles. Nights I would lie awake in bed and review my shift, reliving memories of customers who had been kind or awful, calculating how much each had left me, trying to figure out what had gone right or wrong. How was it strangers saw me? What made them decide to reward or punish? Disaster nights I shivered in recovery, emotionally damaged from the abuses of softball leagues and Toastmasters.

I didn't want to admit it, but restaurant work had the feeling of permanence. In college, I worked at a few bistros and learned what a wine list can do for tips. The first night I broke $100 at a yuppie seafood place (back when mesquite wood and blackened fish were a revelation), I was ecstatic. Giddy, I zoomed with airplane wings around the parking lot of my apartment complex, and then, like any good restaurant worker, went and spent my haul at a bar. I cycled through different places, quitting during finals because school was the supposed priority, but if someone told me of an opening, I ran over in a pressed white shirt and black pants, drawn by the fast cash, instant drama, icy cocktails and the sharp, restless banter of restaurant people—my people.

Postgraduation I tried to find that ever-elusive "real" job but failed. I typed and mailed out resumes but should have spent the postage money on lottery tickets. I started temping and learned that fluorescent lighting, combined with eight hours of mind-numbing imprisonment, made me wonder if my neck might fit under the paper cutter. After a few miserable months transcribing and filing, I walked down the street to the Mexican restaurant where I would remain for the next three years. Each month I swore was my last, that I would fulfill the promise of my honors degree from a top university. Every few nights I would melt down over a customer and wind up sobbing in the walk-in cooler. For many reasons (poor memory, possible dyslexia, smart mouth, hypersensitivity and the aforementioned social anxiety), I wasn't a natural, but at least waiting tables paid a living wage and featured ambient lighting. I didn't have to sit still, and I worked with other people who couldn't sit still, meaning I had friends. While everyone I knew lived for Sundays, I mulled over my book and drank coffee every morning. Around thirty hours a week is considered full time, so I could play in bands and renovate my house, and while the work is intense, it flies by.

The problem was while tip money paid the rent, I craved a sense of vocation, a job that people respected. Waiters are all waiting for something. Waiters might be waiting to finish school, or waiting to go back to school, or waiting for their band to break, or waiting to open their own restaurant, or waiting to get home to their kids, or waiting for their catering/jewelry design/massage therapy business to take off—but no waiter is only a waiter. Cooks and even chefs often make less money, but their position is one of more esteem. Waiters are the lowest of the restaurant chain, the necessary evil, the charlatans, the used car salesmen, the snake oil vinaigrette on the food service salad. Waiting is a means to an end, a trading of your honest opinion for cash, a form of prostitution. The situation remains acceptable so long as people are sane, but vindictive miscreants cycle through, and when they do, you aren't just expected to rise above, but to polish their dirty plates with your black tie. Suffering abuse as a law enforcement officer or medical professional is an act of nobility, but where, really, is the honor in placating some self-entitled fop over his filet mignon? Some nights I went home and no amount of hot water could rinse the ick.

In 1993, I went into therapy with one goal: to get out of restaurant work. I sat on the purple plush loveseat and told the moon-faced therapist I was here so she could help me "get out of the business." Waiters often talk about "getting out" as if we served martinis in Alcatraz.

"Interesting," she said. "And why does restaurant work bother you?"

Zing. Of course, waiting tables is a "real" job, ask anyone who has done it. Yet, in my family, an unspoken yet understood article of faith was that my great-grandparents did not immigrate in search of a new life so my grandfather could work in a toll booth, so my mother could be the first generation to attend college, and marry a man who endured a Catholic orphanage, so he could join the Navy, which would pay for college, so he could become a college professor, so his daughter could have the same conversation fifty times a night four times a week over the course of three years.

Kelly: "With your entrée you have a choice of black beans, pinto beans, rice or the daily vegetable, which is zucchini."

Customer: "And what is the daily vegetable?"

Kelly: "Zucchini."

Customer: "What comes with the entrée?"

I swear I wasn't the Family Disappointment on purpose. When I met people who said they were editors, or graphic designers, or environmental scientists or did blahdy blah for one of the many companies in Research Triangle Park, I clutched at the envy cramp in my chest. My former college roommates became Wall Street stockbrokers, college professors, rape victim advocates, lawyers, biologists and, yes, doctors. My brother is a rocket scientist. No, really. Somehow, everyone knew how to flip this job raspberry but me.

Please don't ask if I've ever read *What Color Is Your Parachute.*

One of the greatest regrets of my twenties was turning down a job at the Hillsborough newspaper. The position, small-town southern reporter, was a dream job at the time, work I really wanted—a potential vocation. The hitch was it paid a third of what I made waiting tables, and there was no way to keep a few shifts and take this job. Crunch time I folded, an anxiety attack driving me back to the safety of what I knew.

There are many other stories such as this I could tell.

Over a decade later, I was still in therapy. I would drift off and on the couch, generally drifting back on if I lost a job or broke up with a boyfriend. I had learned a great deal about boundaries, triggers, personal inventories and how family dynamics had shaped my emotional core, all of which improved my quality of life, but I was still waiting tables. One day I made the mistake of asking for my file. I wanted to try and make sense of what, if anything, had happened here. The assistant returned with a sheaf that she heaved onto the counter with a grunt. The paperwork measured over a foot high. Standing in the long shadow of my past, I flipped to the first page, dated July 1993.

Kelly is a young, pleasant woman who comes in seeking treatment in response to a depressive episode. She states her desire to get out of the restaurant business. She seeks a steady relationship and...

I slammed the file shut and left.

My last therapist I only had for three months. She was pregnant and taking a leave, and I decided to take mine with her—the file was thick enough. During a session I was reciting a familiar litany of woes before I stopped talking midsentence. I was boring the both of us. We fell silent.

"Well," she said, clasping her hands over her round belly, "it sounds as though if you want a change, you are going to have to take a risk."

Take a risk.

Sometimes words cut through you. You could have heard these words a thousand times, but one day they take hold. For whatever reason, on this day, these words cut through me. There was simply no way for me to move forward without gambling that life might get worse. This didn't mean I had to bet my life savings on a horse named Bamboozle, but if I wanted to change, then I would have to risk.

A few weeks after that, I was sitting on the front porch of my little blue house, staring at the oak tree, reading *Silver Lake*.

The night before I left for Montana, I drank my last shots with my last restaurant gang on my last restaurant shift. On my way out I tossed my stained apron and worn Doc Martens in the dumpster. I exhaled the final sweet stink of rotted meat in the North Carolina summer.

Total count: twenty years.

A covered wagon pulled by two horses jangled across the skyline of short grass and prairie clover. I wound down a gravel road, past farmland punctuated with round bales of hay, and nestled once again amongst the minivans. I'd never thought of my gray, four-door sedan as "sporty" before, but in the rural Midwest, my Camry was a James Bond car. In the parking lot, I counted at least three sets of little Marys and Lauras in their respective blue and red dresses, bouncing around like calico jumping beans. The "Ingalls Homestead" was indeed located on the original Ingalls Homestead, although the property did not include the site of the original claim shanty, which was owned by the Memorial Society. I could see the historical marker over a coulee, surrounded by the original cottonwoods Pa planted. To my right was the Ingalls Homestead replica claim shanty, with the replica cottonwoods.

I went in, purchased my ticket and adhered a neon green sticker that read "Ingalls Homestead—Laura's Living Prairie" to my white apron. The word *living*, I noticed, directly contrasted the word *memorial*.

This tour was self-guided. I held out my brightly colored, cartoon map and set out to explore the various historically inspired outbuildings. There was the claim shanty, but also a sod house, stable, viewing tower and little white schoolhouse. Black holes dotted the mowed prairie with gophers popping in and out as if they were paid staff—the combined effect being that of a giant, pioneer-themed putt-putt golf course. At my feet, a gopher with glittering black eyes jumped up and dared me catch him. I took the bait and wound up swiping the air. Pa had battled these critters in his attempts to raise a corn crop. The gophers, it appeared, had emerged victorious.

The Ingalls Homestead was geared for kids. There were pioneer learning games, horses to pet and hands-on crafts. Here I hit yet another pioneer pothole, in that I wasn't sure where I fit in. Single adults can't smack kids aside and take a turn, but if you have kids, then it's okay to smack other kids aside for the sake of your kid. Parents, unlike singletons, get to join in, because they are "supervising" or "spending quality time together," and I began to have a new appreciation for the desire to raise a family.

At the stable, a freckled Dakota boy in suspenders led us through the pioneer activities.

"Do you need any help supervising?" I offered.

"Oh, don't worry about that. It's all pretty easy, and the kids catch on quick."

"No, no. I want to," I insisted, squeezing his arm maybe a little firmer than necessary.

The kids and I got to work. We braided rope and sang "Git Along Little Dogies" as we play-lassoed. We stroked the forelocks of the gentle horses, Pet and Patty, and squealed over mewling gray barn kittens. We ground wheat in the coffee grinder to make coarse, brown bread for the long winter and twisted hay into sticks for fuel. The girls and I made corncob dolls, just like Laura had in *Big Woods*, while the boys made corncob superheroes.

I turned to a pair of sisters dressed like Laura and Mary. All three of us were fussing over which square of cloth to use.

"Would you rather make a corncob superhero? Because you can, if you want," I said.

"No," they said in unison.

"You know, Laura helped Pa on the farm with chores that boys usually did and—"

Here I wisely stopped myself before I launched into a lecture on gender bias.

"—Your dolls are cool. I like what you've done there with the red."

"Thank you," they said. A boy zipped around the barn, flying his limbless corn hero.

Crafts accomplished, we rode in a covered wagon, taking turns holding the reigns of Pet and Patty. It only took this short journey for me to learn the harsh realities of travel via prairie schooner. Prairies are generally thought of as flat, and I suppose they are, compared to the Rocky Mountains, but they are not flat compared to a paved road. The wagon bounced and jostled, and despite the modern, rubber tires installed to absorb the shock, it wasn't long before my rear end had been drubbed into the consistency of overworked dough. My next read of *Little House*, when Laura describes her body aching from wagon rides while perched on a wooden plank, would take place with a new appreciation.

The wagon let us off at a little white schoolhouse on a knoll. The bell rang, and we filed in our wooden desks. A teacher up front led us in activities, and we solved a Mother Goose riddle.

In marble walls as white as milk,
Lined with a skin as soft as silk,
Within a fountain crystal clear,
A golden apple doth appear.

No doors there are to this stronghold,
Yet thieves break in and steal the gold.[2]

The kids sang and performed a little march around the room while we all snapped pictures and laughed. School is great if you only have to stay for ten minutes.

The arena of school, first as a student and then as a teacher, becomes Laura's proving ground for the last two books of the series. She makes best girlfriends Ida Brown, Mary Power and Minnie Johnson. She shows she can still take down a rival when, in a classic rematch, Nellie Oleson reappears. Most significantly, school becomes Laura's professional test; she needs to do well so she can pass her boards, teach and help send Mary to college. For the higher goal she must learn to negotiate her independent spirit with the responsibilities of adulthood. The second character in this drama isn't Nellie, who remains a worthy, if somewhat one-dimensional opponent, but Laura's future sister-in-law, Eliza Jane Wilder.

Miss Wilder's term teaching quickly turns to disaster. She cannot manage a frontier classroom and has it out for the Ingalls girls. Laura, in return, doesn't mean to be immature and encourage classroom anarchy, but little actions keep spiraling into larger ones. The situation deteriorates until it bottoms out. Laura takes the low road when she pens a nifty rhyme that soon has all the schoolboys chanting "lazy, lousy, Lizy Jane" up and down Main Street, revealing to the entire town the teacher's humiliating secret that once, as a girl, she was sent home with lice.

Not a year later, Laura faces her karma in another classroom, this time from the other side of the podium. The first instance her class turns unruly, in a flash she realizes that this was how Miss Wilder felt. It's not so easy to manage a classroom filled with ungrateful beasts who can turn a spelling bee into a mosh pit. Now Laura understands the pressures Miss Wilder was under from the students, from her employer, from the parents, and how if she failed, she might have to pack up and go back East—meaning utter humiliation.

And now, so did I.

---

[2] Answer: An egg.

When I left North Carolina, I quit my last restaurant job. What next? You may have wondered. The product of two teachers and lifelong Laurafan, I suppose I always saw my vocation coming down the blackboard pipe, inevitable as the Norton Anthologies on my bookshelf and pilled cardigan sweaters amassing in my bureau.

Was I a better schoolteacher than waiter? It was hard to say. I could vouch that it was a freaky feeling to walk in front of the classroom and realize mine was the seat up front. Also surreal: a roomful of people staring, expecting you to be some kind of expert. Laura captures perfectly the awkward social situation of teaching, how a bad class resembles an Alcoholics Anonymous meeting without coffee. My previous public speaking experience had been limited to a recitation of the daily specials. When I first heard the sound of my own voice droning on and on, all I could think was, *Why doesn't that woman shut up?* When I first began teaching freshman composition at the University of Montana, I often suspected I was experiencing the revenge of Miss Wilder; I enjoyed her demise a little too much. As fate would have it, I was a lazy, lousy disciplinarian. I liked to believe this was because I created an "open dialogue" with my students, but when I found myself regularly banging my textbook on the podium like a gavel, I had to wonder.

In the movies, students are angry, and the teachers are psychological judo masters who channel this intense emotion into a desire to read poetry and pass Advanced Placement exams. I found my greatest classroom battle was with apathy. Every day I punched a pillow until my arms gave out.

But even as I griped, I knew that the cardigan fit, and I would wear it.

I was no longer waiting.

On my way out, I snagged a few more items at the gift shop to add to my growing pile. By way of making conversation, I mentioned to the cashier that I had seen the Surveyors' House that morning, leaving out the part about getting snubbed, but somehow she knew.

"Wasn't this fun?" she asked, giving me a knowing look as she rang me up (postcards, a fiddle magnet, more books, a bonnet for my niece). "Here we let you *touch* things."

I nodded politely as I handed her my credit card, although I wasn't sure I agreed. That's the problem with trying to connect with your dream world. I wanted to pick up the Surveyors' House and put it back out where it belonged, surrounded by prairie, buffalo wolves and the Big Slough with great winged birds flying overhead and not a soul for miles. But Silver Lake was now a sewage pool and the Big Slough a Fair-to-Middlin'-Sized Slough. There was no way for me to have what I wanted, unless I put the Books down on the floor and somehow jumped inside them.

Before getting back in my car, I walked over to the plaque that commemorated the original shanty. The original cottonwoods Pa planted for each one of his girls hadn't grown so much as endured. The limbs, bent from years of prairie winds, sprawled arthritically upward, looking more like giant sagebrush than trees.

But they were alive.

I stood where the claim shanty would have been.

Here, I thought. *Right here.*

On my way back to the Prairie Manor, I bought another banana crème pie Blizzard from Dairy Queen for dinner. After nights of hamburgers, hot dogs and heat lamp pizza, vegetables were pretty much a mysterious food from the past, so I figured I'd focus on calcium intake. I took the Blizzard up to my room at the Prairie Manor and poured a mini bottle of Sutter Home chardonnay over ice.

Laura concluded her first job basting shirts with a total of nine dollars to put toward Mary's college fund. Even her boss, Mrs. White, had to admit that Laura could beat her making buttonholes. Laura didn't enjoy sitting hunched over all day in a chair, yet when she was let go, she was disappointed, feeling that somehow she had not done enough. A depression set in.

"Nine dollars is nothing to sneeze at," said Pa. "You've done good work, too, and fully satisfied Mrs. White, haven't you?"

"Yes," Laura answered honestly.

"Then it's a good job well done."

In my past restaurant life, many was the night I stocked cases of wine, hauled tray after tray of plates, worked past the point of exhaustion, took extra shifts, worked doubles, juggled two (or more) jobs, picked up that last table that rolled in at closing and went on when all I wanted in the world was to give up and go home. I had my meltdown nights (chocolate cake, coconut cake), but more often I managed a staggering number of tasks that required the right balance of physical coordination and emotional intelligence. People say everyone should wait tables for a summer, but that's not nearly enough. After twenty years, I was still learning about how humans behave, how we are kind and evil and funny and sad. From restaurant work I am so skilled at gauging facial expressions, it's as though I can read minds, words broadcasting like ticker tape across people's foreheads. Restaurant people develop a heightened sense of awareness that makes other people seem mealy.

I had paid my way in the world and done my best, and it was time I made peace with the apron.

Then it's a good job well done.

I toasted my restaurant career with the screw-cap wine.

Thanks, Pa.

A bane of the waiter's life is the recurring waiter nightmare that haunts long after the job is over. Mine always takes place at the restaurant I worked the longest, eight years. The computer won't function. Entrées I can't reach congeal under the heat lamp. Chefs bellow. I flip through my ticket book over and over desperately trying to decipher illegible orders. This gerbil wheel scurrying goes on and on until at some point, guided by some neural pattern, I push open the emergency exit door—which leads to a Superdome-sized dining room of furious customers who all need water and bread. Often my waiter dream morphs into other bad dreams, that I'm failing a test, running away, naked, losing my teeth, trying to save kittens, falling.

Snuggled in my quilt, reading *Golden Years* in preparation for tomorrow, I knew none of these night demons would haunt me tonight. I read a study once that it's difficult to study people who have nightmares because once they enroll in a sleep clinic, they sleep soundly through the night. The theory is they feel watched over, protected. This was the effect De Smet had on me. At the Prairie House Manor, with keys taped on the door, I slept the deep sleep of the secure.

Chapter Ten
Over Thirty-Five with Cats

De Smet, South Dakota: *These Happy Golden Years*

What do men have to do to be men? Sleep with a woman. Kill something. Yes, killing something, some luckless deer, duck, bear, pretty much anything large-ish in the animal kingdom, or even another man, appropriate in times of war, has ushered many a lad into manhood. But what's a woman to do? She gets to want to have a baby.

—Joy Williams, "The Case Against Babies"

As I entered my thirties, friends disappeared like the cast of a murder mystery. I lost them to spouses, day jobs and—the final good-bye—children. I'd make plans with breeders only to find myself covered in ketchup and home by 8 o'clock. To have a social life, I found it necessary to befriend people much younger. I knew they would also marry, procreate and abandon me, but I figured by then my original friends would have divorced and sent their kids to college.

One evening I was sitting in a circle of young women, no one over the age of twenty-five, discussing relationships. They weren't ready to settle down but didn't want to wait *too* long.

"God," the mouthy one said. She was too worldly for this life—Europe had changed her. "The worst thing in the world is winding up over thirty-five with cats."

I batted my eyelashes and did my best to pass for thirty-four. Looking down, I realized my black shirt had the texture of orange tabby mohair.

I was every young woman's fear.

Once upon a time I, too, believed in relationship scheduling. I remember when "settling down" was something marked on a Hello Kitty! calendar by a sticker. "Marriage" was penciled in for the late twenties followed by a few years of world travel together. Somehow, between sojourns to Paris and Thailand, careers would be established and real estate acquired. Then, and only then, would the 2.3 children enter the picture, a few years apart, one boy and one girl, with the .3's gender generously up for grabs.

I've noticed life doesn't always shake down this way.

Even so, most people seem to manage the married and procreating gig by a certain age, and those who don't are suspect, especially if said person is venturing through uberconservative areas such as rural Kansas, Minnesota and South Dakota. Many times on my trip I felt a little tense, the oddity of being the not-young-nor-old woman traveling alone. While the world is filled with maverick women adventurers, these lone she-wolves are out skateboarding the Great Wall of China or surfing in Fiji. They aren't driving two-lane highways through the Corn Belt.

The vast majority of Laura pilgrims were families. During my entire trip I did not see one solo woman traveler. Not one. The two college students were the only women I met roadtripping together (aside from the Amish in Pepin and a tour bus of Golden Girls at the pageant, both of whom had male drivers). I was a curiosity at best, a threat to American values at worst. I was thirty-eight, almost thirty-nine. If we are to believe the hype, around that age a woman's plumbing shuts down like a Detroit manufacturing plant. It's time to give up the ghost, let the gray take over, adopt a thousand cats, live in a ramshackle house, and let your love life consist of underlined passages in *Wuthering Heights*.

Having been both in and out of relationships, I could vouch that it was easy to romanticize a man when you didn't have to deal with one. Still, and I really, really hated to admit this, it was difficult to be single and in my thirties and not feel as though I had failed on some level. There was not only the lost love, but the shame. *What's wrong with you?*

When I was a teenager, family and friends waved their hands, dismissing my misgivings about men and marriage. I'd get the ole wink and pinch. *Of course* I was going to meet that special someone, and as for pregnancy, I would "change my mind." Around my early twenties people remained indulgent, but I could see a worry crease starting to bisect the forehead. By my late twenties the vibe was, "Okay, get on with it now." I can vouch that by a woman's late thirties, no one winks and asks coyly about the boyfriend or the babies anymore. The small talkers fear the answer. I might be transitioning into a man, heretic, divorced, widowed, dying, sterile or cursed with chronic bacterial vaginosis. Whatever the reason, it was probably poor afternoon tea conversation. Better not go there.

Here I was, staring down the barrel of forty. I had never been especially hung up on age, but there are moments when a woman has to realize certain undertakings are no longer possible. (Quite possibly, I might have to accept that I will never be an Olympic figure skater.) I'd already aged out of the rock star career. There came the day when I pulled out the silver sparkle pants I used to wear onstage and said to myself, *no más, señorita*. If I was going to settle down, well, maybe I should start to worry a little bit.

My Manly had arrived on his brown Morgan horse the stroke before midnight. The timing was like one of those twists of fate people talk about, as though life and love were just as everyone had ever said—that I would know when I was ready, and then, and only then, would the right person turn up. It was easier, telling people I was in a relationship. I was one of the gang, blended, an even number. Part of the fun of Laura and Almanzo's courtship was that everyone was paired off. Mary Power and Cap Garland. Minnie Johnson and Fred Gilbert. Frank Harthorn and May Bird. Arthur Johnson and some girl Laura did not know—even that girl had a date.

I had traded the pronoun *I* for *we*. What are we having for dinner? What movie should we watch? What should we do for the holidays? What I didn't know was whether My Manly and I were a we etched in stone or a we scribbled on a cocktail napkin. In the twenty-first-century relationship comes the point when every couple must ask, is this love or are we just hanging out?

Laura and Almanzo's courtship revolved around Sunday drives—cutters in the winter and buggies in the spring—the nineteenth-century version of cruising. Laura and Almanzo had particular lakes that were scenes of their courtship—Lake Thompson, Lake Henry and Spirit Lake. Over a series of Sundays, they carved out a route. Manly would pick Laura up and they'd ride south across bare prairie to lakes Henry and Thompson, along the narrow neck of land between, then over the prairie again to north of Spirit Lake fifteen miles away. Forty or fifty miles in all, but always, as Laura put it, "around the square" to come home. My intention was to retrace the route of Almanzo and Laura's Sunday buggy drive. Lakes Thompson and Henry were a short drive back east on Highway 14, so I headed in that direction first.

My high school boyfriend, Mike, and I had our own loop: down MacFarland Boulevard, right on Highway 65 through downtown Tuscaloosa to Northport, and finally "around the square" to land at the Krispy Kreme. Often we'd detour out to Lake Tuscaloosa and stare out on the flat, brown expanse, hoping. Hoping for what, we had no idea. The source of angst defied capture. If you asked me now I'd say we hoped for escape, for a life more than this, for a love that could save us from our dull, suburban existence. We were hoping because life was too boring not to hope. A lake was the only place that could absorb all this intense need, the water functioning like a nuclear plant cooling tower.

As I got closer to the lake, the arid, yellow prairie morphed into bright green bogs with thick-growing reeds. Flocks of birds flew over the marshes and watchful egrets stood on one leg. The Ingalls family witnessed a decimation of the bird population—probably Pa shooting enough for a feather bed didn't help. Modern hunting regulations meant the bird population had a chance to rebuild, and not for the first time, I saw how hunters are some of the most motivated ecologists around. Laura never describes an egret. I wondered if she ever saw one.

The road dead-ended at Lake Thompson, and I stepped out. I don't know what I had expected, but this was no puddle. The opposite shore was a thin line in the distance, the land barely visible to my left and right. Before me the silver water beckoned, rippled and wild, as though a portal to some primeval world. I half-expected Nessie's head to surface, a living relic from the Cretaceous Sea.

Waves lapped fast and furious, sounds of the ocean on meth, the ever-present wind rushing across the water. Giant, white-winged birds squawked over the churning backbeat. I stood on the gravelly shore, my hair and skirts whipping around, and I couldn't help but think, *Man, do I need kissing.* My Manly should be here so we could clutch one another beneath the desolate, scrubby trees. I would wear a lilac dress and My Manly a brown suit, like my beloved cover of *Golden Years*, my hand demurely outstretched to his.

"Your hand is so small," My Manly would murmur. "I was wondering. Perhaps it would like an engagement ring."

"Then it would depend on who gave the ring," I would slyly rejoin, just as Laura had, to let Almanzo know she was no easy conquest.

My father was twenty-six and my mother twenty-one when they married, my mother seventeen years younger than I was now. In the black-and-white wedding portrait that sits on my dresser, my parents look so young it's shocking, as though their bones haven't quite set. My brother and sister-in-law were high school sweethearts. They met at age fifteen, box-stepped at the Snowflake Dance and have been together ever since. Laura married at eighteen. I had never cared to marry that young, but if part of the marriage allure is sharing a life, you have to meet early enough so there is life left to share.

My life was halfway over.

Marrying young means that as you both droop, you have shared memories of firmer flesh. When the eighty-year-old man gooses his eighty-year-old wife and says, "She looks the same as the day we met!" while she giggles like a schoolgirl, there's a part of him that is telling the truth. Memory plays games with perception. Ma, in an effort to nudge Laura into wearing her corsets, was fond of reminding Laura that when she married her Pa, he could span her waist with his two hands. Laura's saucy retort was that Pa still seemed to like her well enough now. People tend to remember one another looking as how they met. If my husband was going to remember me as young, I was running out of time.

Husband. The word sat thick and strange on my lips, and still conjured feelings of mild panic and an impulse to scan for Exit signs, but there it was. Adulthood should have cured me of romance—tales of adultery, lies, theft, abuse, passive-aggressive Post-it wars, bed deaths, bed burnings. By never marrying in the first place, I told myself, I had escaped marriage tragedy.

But it might've been nice to be asked.

The hair lashing my face began to feel more irritating than romantic. With no one to kiss, my thoughts turned to food. The North Shore Bar and Grill offered views of the lake and the possibility of my first sit-down meal in a while. The interior decor of blue chairs, rubber tablecloths and cruets reminded me of bayside restaurants of the 1970s Gulf Coast. From the bartender I learned that Lake Thompson didn't used to be so tremendous. It had grown a great deal twenty years ago when rainstorms flooded the area, and many people lost their property.

The baked walleye was buttery and flaky. Lake Thompson technically had walleye, a nonnative fish stocked for sport, but my meal was from Canada. Because of inspection regulations, the bartender said.

A man said he had been to the Sioux City Zoo, but it was nothing much to see. Not like the one in Omaha. The sad animals in cages depressed him, he said, and he was sorry he took his kids there.

"Sioux City," the bartender said. "It's trying."

"Ha, ha," the bartender and man laughed dryly and exchanged knowing glances. I didn't respond, as I had never been either place.

I have no excuse for my long, lame history of relationship woes. Laura taught me all I ever needed to know.

First: Know his family.

People say you can't choose your family, but marriage is the one instance we do. Witness the difference between the Wilder and the Ingalls families, versus the Olesons or the Brewsters. Choose wisely. When adult Almanzo reappears in the series, we already know a great deal from meeting his strict but loving and highly capable parents in *Farmer Boy*. Almanzo comes from a family that prioritizes a work ethic, honesty and big meals.

Second: Is he kind to animals?

Out and out animal cruelty is a natural deal breaker, and the recent studies that link animal abuse to human abuse come as no big shock. I would argue that indifference is also worth our scrutiny. Some people claim they are too busy and can't be bothered, or treat animals like machines at their disposal. A man who would leave his horse out in the cold is a man who would shove children on his way to the last Titanic lifeboat. Almanzo proves time and again he is conscientious with his stock. He would never tease and ruin a colt. Almanzo knows how to earn an animal's trust, so he will understand the daily nurturing required of an enduring love. This is the man who will arrive every Friday to pick you up from the Brewster school. And bring you back every Sunday afternoon.

Third: Relationships must be based in honesty.

During Laura's tenure at the Brewster school, Laura feels guilty that Almanzo is driving so far in the cold every weekend because she (at the time) has no romantic intentions. She wrestles with her conscience. Despite her desperate desire for a ride home, she doesn't want to lead Almanzo on. So she comes clean, informs him that she will not ride with him once her school term is over, which leads us to—

Fourth: Follow through.

Almanzo's reply lets us know he's a keeper. Indignant, he lets her know that he is not the kind of fellow to strand her at Brewster's, when she's so lonely and homesick, due to his selfishness. The adult female reader might know that men don't drive their horses through forty below Dakota winters to play pinochle. Nonetheless, Almanzo doesn't pout and give up. A lesser man might. There's the time to take a hint, but in the meantime a person needs to fulfill his promise. A great partner understands that implied promises are just as important. I don't know that love means never having to say you're sorry, but you shouldn't have to ask for what you need all the time. People who love you know what you need.

Fifth: He should be a good tipper.

When the Wilders marry, Almanzo tips the Reverend Brown ten dollars. That's a nineteenth-century ten dollars. A man who is generous with others will be generous with you. My years waiting tables confirmed this lesson. Whenever I saw a man taking a woman out to dinner and the woman was miserable, the subsequent miserly tip was predictable. This man, by the way, is inevitably the man who tells you what a great tipper he is.

Sixth: Character.

Laura shows us that Almanzo is a man of mettle, honesty and capability. Character is the stuff of a lifetime. It's easy to promise for better and worse while pounds of grilled shrimp and Champagne await. But what about car wrecks, foreclosure, cancer? Almanzo and Laura are the people you want around when the locust plague hits.

This is not to say you will spend all your days together bathed in a golden light.

Rose wrote her mother a letter once, wanting details from her father about his trek west to the Dakotas for her novel *Free Land*.

"As for getting Manly to tell what someone said—Have you heard of oysters?" Laura replied, referring to Almanzo's taciturn, clammed up ways.

Oh, how I knew of Laura's struggle to maintain conversation with a bivalve mollusk. My Manly absorbed sound like a Sealy Posturepedic. Before our dates I would mentally review topics of discussion, and when alone I would parse the verbal tidbits, attempting to decode how our evening went. I admit that sometimes the silence made me nervous, as though I must be this horribly boring person.

Laura didn't mind Almanzo's quietude once she understood that it wasn't her. Laura didn't need small talk. What she needed was a physical presence that made her feel safe. She needed to look outside the shanty on Sunday and know she could count on the buggy coming across the prairie. She needed someone who, when he set out to do a job, took care of every detail, no slacking. She needed someone who made her feel better just by being in the room.

I had to admit, the silences between My Manly and I weren't always comfortable. I monologued to fill the space until I ran out of material, at which point I stopped midstream and sighed. Often I was later compelled to apologize and email, "Sorry I came over with rambly mouth again. I felt better after spewing even though I think I had told you each one of those stories about twenty times."

To which My Manly would reply, "I like your rambly mouth. And kissing your rambly mouth."

Every Friday Manly showed up, and having him around brought me peace. If I wanted to talk, I decided, that's why I had women friends.

I thought finding Spirit Lake would be simple enough, that I'd drive north of town and encounter a Sign, but as it turned out, continent-sized glaciers from ten thousand years ago were out to foil my plans. The Wisconsonian glaciation covered the Great Plains in continent-sized sheets of ice, bringing rocks and minerals from as far as Hudson Bay, pulverizing limestone, shale, quartzite, granite and hornblende into Pa's beloved soil. When the glacier rescinded, lakes remained scattered all over this area of the Great Plains.

What this meant for me was the more I drove the more I found lakes. I would see a body of water, pull over and jump up and down shouting, "Sprit Lake! Sprit Lake!" Then I would drive and see another lake. I don't know if I ever found the real Spirit Lake, but I knew what it was like to go on long buggy rides free of town, free of prying adult eyes, free of expectations. I wished that Mike and I could have driven to these Spirit Lakes. Lake Tuscaloosa was a man-made murky affair, with snakes and insects lurking in the brown squishy mud. The rocky, lustrous Dakota lakes inspired clarity of mind.

On one of my turnoffs, I found a little white church with a little white steeple, on a grassy hillside. One glance showed that this was a cared-for community center. I could practically smell fried chicken and pie. I meant to simply pause and look, but before I could stop myself I was Bridget Jonesing, off in a fantasy flash.

My Manly and I stand at the door, holding hands and waving, me in pioneer wedding dress and My Manly in a nineteenth-century suit. No, wait. I am in black cashmere just as Laura wore, sewn exactly as Laura describes. No, the brown poplin and a poke bonnet with the ostrich feathers that fly off in the wind. Down by the feathery green trees awaits a black buggy drawn by two brown Morgan horses. I have packed my trousseau: petticoats, bustles, a polonaise, a lace jabot. Chemises! I have chemises! My friends and family stroll the lawn in pioneer costume. Everyone deems South Dakota as the best place for a destination wedding ever. Long tables covered in red-checked tablecloths are filled with crispy salt pork, fluffy sourdough biscuits, green tomatoes in yogurt, apples 'n' onions and vanity cakes. Afterwards, My Manly and I ride off to a little gray house with custom-made cabinetry. I unpack the crisp, white hand-stitched muslin sheets…

And, stop. Was this scene really my dream? Maybe. Maybe not. Either way, this vision was pretty much the opposite of me standing alone in rural South Dakota, wearing a dress that could double as a bridesmaid's nightmare. My Manly and I had made up before the trip, but remained on sketchy ground at best. I knew better than to even discuss commitment, much less the *M* word. We were supposed to be too modern for that.

I drove back downtown. There was a little white house near the Prairie Manor with a FOR SALE sign that I had been stalking over the past few days. I would walk over and sneak around the property, taking mental inventory of how I would renovate and landscape. Admittedly, I have what could be termed a "little house" problem, in that I want to buy, fix up and live in every one I see. I went by for another visit and even wrote down the phone number. The yard was scraggly and the paint chipped, but the bay window and Victorian porch beckoned. I could even see surviving the Dakota winter with a fireplace, insulated windows and stack of *Youth's Companion* magazines. But no way could I hack it alone.

The De Smet pageant was performed outdoors near the Ingalls homestead. Laura pilgrims and locals filtered down to the theater, a hustle-bustle of town spirit descending on the Plains. The set was less elaborate than Walnut Grove but featured the borrowed natural landscape, yellow prairie stretching off in every direction with a blanket of blue sky on top. A store, a living room, a church and a school formed a dollhouse stage, homestead shanties missing a wall. Foot-stomping fiddle music played over the speakers while a covered wagon circled the grounds chased by flocks of children, bonnet strings flying.

At the gate I was handed a tabloid, *These Happy Golden Years News,* that featured profiles of the cast, Ingalls family bios, a list of scenes ("Brewster School," "A Talk with Mary," etc.), and results of the LIW Society Middle School Contest. The essay winner was Elizabeth Schlosser, who concluded her piece, "Our lives may be totally different, but I think that all girls have a little prairie girl just waiting to come out."

I looked down at my toes peeking out from the orange flounce and fluffed my skirts. Schlosser made a compelling argument.

The front page featured an article on the local attractions, recommending the Laura Ingalls Wilder Society for "the history buff," and the Ingalls Homestead "for the young at heart." The first pageant had been held at the high school auditorium in 1955. The tradition had taken off from there, and in 1974 the Pageant Society purchased thirty acres. Now there was a corresponding show for each of the Books set in De Smet. This year's pageant was *These Happy Golden Years*, "adapted for the stage by Tom Roberts and based on original material by Marian Cramer."

For seating, rows of wooden slabs had been propped on cinder blocks to create makeshift bleachers, and many had brought lawn chairs or quilts. I spread out my Ozark quilt, reclined and watched the skyline change from cornflower to hot white, the sun not going gently into that good night. Across the prairie, a teenage couple with androgynous long hair dressed in thrift store couture walked hand in hand—the two lone hipsters of all the Dakotas. His mop top and her dyed auburn hair stood out amidst the careful corn-colored coiffures. Their shadow silhouettes trailed behind, long and dark against the pale grass. The couple seemed excited, imbued with purpose. Their hands flapped, animated in conversation, their strides long and fast. I imagined them plotting their great escape after high school. Minneapolis, perhaps. Or Portland, Oregon. Mike and I had once gripped hands and dreamed of escape from Tuscaloosa. In 1886, we probably would have married, but in 1986, it was unthinkable that either of us would change our college plans for a relationship. That would be ghetto.

The pageant had a similar narrative structure to the one in Walnut Grove, with Laura the elderly narrator reflecting back on her childhood, or in this case, young adulthood. As the scenes unfolded,

I couldn't help but nurture the fantasy that I would return next summer, live in my little white house, get a job working at Ingalls Homestead and audition for a role in the pageant. Although then I couldn't figure out my part. I was too old to play teenage Laura and too young to play elderly narrator Laura. I wasn't exactly the Ma type. Mrs. Oleson? No, thanks. The role of Mrs. Brewster, though, could be cool, if I got to wield a butcher knife behind the curtain à la *Psycho*.

That part wasn't in the pageant.

The actor playing Almanzo, Matthew Sheridan, was a sixteen-year-old junior who liked reading and computers. His goal was to be an archaeologist. Kristen Aanenson was a fifteen-year-old sophomore whose interests included cheerleading, church theater and oral interpretation. Throughout the performance, Laura and Almanzo's voices rang high-pitched over the prairie. Watching actual teenagers play the roles of Laura and Almanzo made me realize how young they had been. Pageant Almanzo's glued-on moustache perched on his upper lip like a hamster. I had always been aware that Laura was fifteen when Almanzo stopped by for that first cutter ride, but it was different watching this age in action. The actress who played Laura put a bit more melodrama into her role than Laura ever did, a bit disconcerting, although probably more realistic. Throughout the *Golden Years* book, Laura never loses her cool, not even when Nellie threatens to steal her suitor's affections. There is a scene where Laura is teaching and wondering if Almanzo will show up that Sunday. "If he didn't; he didn't; that was all," she muses while staring coolly out the window.

If he didn't, he didn't? That's not how I remembered my teenage self. Mike and I enacted emotional dramas that put Telemundo to shame. We would drive and cry and park and scream and cry and drive. I suspected Laura's storytelling reflected her mature years. Or it could be modern teenagers are less mature than pioneer ones. Back then, the concept of "teenager" didn't exist. People went straight from childhood to adulthood, with very few buggy rides in between.

Onstage, Nellie Oleson inserted herself in the courtship buggy, right between Almanzo and Laura. She squealed and flapped her hands as the audience roared. In both pageants, whenever Nellie took the stage the crowd sprung to life.

The sky was black polished glass. The night air began to snap, and I snuggled in my quilt. The scattered audience formed a mirror constellation to the array of stars above. We all knew how this story ended, but that didn't stop us from clapping wildly as Laura once again fended off Nellie and married her one true love.

My final morning in De Smet, I signed the Prairie Manor guest book *Laura Elizabeth Ingalls* and patted each daybed good-bye; they had been good to me. I drove by the little white house one last time. It reminded me of the little blue house I had left in Durham. I suppose that's why I had formed such a quick attachment. Bidding farewell to the De Smet house made me feel connected to Laura. She had left many homes so that she could see what a new place, a new opportunity might offer. On my way out I had one last stop. I parked in front of a historical marker that stood where Laura and Manly's homestead had been. The original buildings were long gone, and the prairie uncultivated. A barbed wire fence blocked the property, and a swell blocked my view, but I opted to respect the barriers this time. I wasn't up for cow wrestling today. Instead I contented myself with the idea that somewhere over there, a long time ago, Laura began her life as an adult.

Nearby grew the remnants of Almanzo's tree claim, a few determined cottonwoods that had stuck it out. Laura's books convey the romance and hopefulness of the nineteenth-century pioneers, but of course many of those dreams never came true. Case in point: the Dakota Forest was never meant to be. Since childhood the Books had sustained me through dark times, Laura's positivity and strength of character functioning as my touchstone. The danger in nostalgia is that by gilding the past, we refuse to take responsibility for our present. Growing up means owning up to the truth. In terms of this trip, this meant I had to connect Laura Ingalls (the character) with Laura Ingalls Wilder (the author), and reconcile this knowledge with the child me who had loved Laura (the character), with the adult me in search of an adult understanding of Laura (both the character and the author), all so that I could somehow, finally, come to an understanding of my own adult self.

That, and I needed to know what was going on with my boyfriend.

When Mary and Laura go for their final evening walk, before Laura moves out, they reminisce about old times. Mary wishes Laura wasn't in such a hurry to move out, but Laura holds fast.

"Yes and what good times we had when we were little," Laura answered. *"But maybe the times that are coming are even better. You never know."*

No, you never did know, but I was going to find out.

CHAPTER ELEVEN
DRIVIN' N' CRYIN'

South Dakota — Nebraska — Kansas

*I have never really felt that I am I; I feel no identification with
myself. My life is not my life but a succession of short stories
and one-act plays, all begun by chance and left unfinished.*
—Rose Wilder Lane, Letters

In 1894, Almanzo and Laura, with their daughter, Rose, embarked upon
their last pioneer journey. They packed up the covered wagon and said
good-bye to Ma, Pa, Mary, Carrie and Grace. The Wilders traveled
south through South Dakota and Nebraska, then headed east, cutting
off the northeast corner of Kansas, angling into southwestern Missouri.
There, in Mansfield, Laura and Almanzo bought Rocky Ridge Farm,
where they lived the rest of their days: Manly, from the age of thirty-
seven until his death at ninety-two, in 1949; and Laura, from the age of
twenty-seven until her death at ninety, in 1957. Mansfield, Missouri,
was my ultimate destination as well.

But first, a bit of driving.

About now the romance of my quest was beginning to fade. I was
supposed to be a dogged Nellie Bly on the investigative trail, hurtling
like a mad comet toward my final homesite. I had a tidy pile of reading
amassed from the gift shops for research, a growing list of unanswered
questions and a supposed epiphany scheduled in which I discovered
how, exactly, a tour of remote Midwestern gift shops in a prairie dress
was going to change my life. All I really wanted was to go home, curl
up with My Manly and watch *Law and Order*.

Twelve days in the same prairie dress might not be much by
nineteenth-century standards, but it was a lot to me. I was at that

point on Halloween night or a wedding when all you want is to change back into your normal clothes, when you feel stupid for having ever called attention to yourself in the first place, and who did you think you were? You might wonder how, in the midst of all this corniferous splendor, Lutheran staring contests and games of cow tag, I had time for laundry. I could have taken a few hours out from my travels, but I was afraid to put the dress in a washing machine. A steady diet of hamburgers, Polish dogs, "broasted" (fried) chicken, heat lamp pizza, Cheetos and DQ Blizzards had made the dress, already cozy and snug, more cozy and snug. One bit of shrinkage and I was done for. Plus, I have always hated washing day. It's probably a childhood scar from the washtub omen of *Silver Lake*.

Laura documented her final pioneer journey in a series of journal entries, later compiled into a published manuscript titled *On the Way Home*. Although rough, the discerning reader can suss out the Laura we know, the writer who through a series of seemingly simple observations crafts a story.

First entry. July 17th, 1894.

> *Started at 8:40 pm. Three miles out, Russian thistles. Harvesters in poor wheat. Crossed the line into Miner Country at 2 o'clock. Camped by a spring that cannot be pumped, but there is feed for the horses. Grain about 8 inches high, will go about 1 ½ bushels to the acre. Hot wind.*

There is a melancholy quality to this prose. I imagine Laura's sorrow at leaving her home, her parents and sisters. In these few lines, the reader experiences a mood (terse, weary), a dark moment (thistles, poor wheat, spring that cannot be pumped) and a hope (feed, grain) before the last sentence casts an unsparing, unsentimental pallor on the entire entry: Hot wind. A mortal might find a way to pump a spring. A mortal can feed the horses. A mortal can grow and sell a crop. But God controls the elements.

From there, Laura's entries turn perfunctory for a while.

We all took a bath.

We started at 8.

We crossed the Kansas River on an iron bridge.

At one point she even describes her frustration to find words. The Wilders encounter some bluffs, and she wishes for an "artist's hand" or a "poet's brain" to be able to describe the scene "in good plain prose."

Laura wanted to capture the spirit of her travels but couldn't find the desire. She must have been exhausted because no writer I know is better at "good plain prose" than LIW. Around mid-Nebraska, I understood her fatigue. The more I drove, the more my brain waves flatlined in response to the landscape. I no longer had observations, romantic or otherwise, to make. The world was me and the road and the dress and the corn. We were all there was.

I drove.

A Story About the Land to Entertain Us Through Nebraska

My high school American history teacher was a Yankee transplant from Ohio, and therefore exotic to us Alabamians. Mr. Nau was not unhandsome with his thick, black hair and lean figure—almost crushable—except he was odd. His teeth were crooked, and his ponderous voice held too much phlegm. He took history seriously in strange ways. At times, he shouted. And he had us all in his thrall.

One day Mr. Nau pulled down a map of the United States. He stared at the middle, so we stared at the middle. Mr. Nau as a rule was ruminative, and even more so this afternoon. Agitated, he paced the room like an overbred racehorse, finger-combing his bristly black hair on end, only to smooth it back down. He lifted his black-framed glasses and pinched the bridge of his nose before his final survey of the troops. He shook his head—oh, what a sorry lot we were.

After what felt like an epoch, Mr. Nau went to the chalkboard and wrote in capital letters: MANIFEST DESTINY.

He waited for us to absorb these words, his expression stone. We exchanged glances and braced for impact. We could smell it coming. Impending was Mr. Nau's Jack Nicholson tirade mode, the stuff of high school legend, eternal fodder for lakeside beer fests and hallway high fives.

Mr. Nau pointed at the board. "*People*," he bobbed the chalk like a goose, "This is the defining concept of our country. It's what shaped who we are today. It's why there are *movie stars* in *Hollywood*. It's why we take our concept of *democracy* abroad. A great portion of our country's character had nothing to do with *men* in *white wigs*, or even *slavery*."

At this he spun on his Oxford-clad heels and gave us southern kids a meaningful look before returning to his lecture.

"There was a greater entity that molded the philosophy of our nation. Greater than the *Declaration of Independence* or even the *Bill of Rights*. It was this…"

He stalked over to the map of North America, hands outreached. "It was *this*…" He motioned over the western half of the United States. "It was *this*!" Mr. Nau spread his hands in a slow dramatic movement, as if to massage the Rockies.

Mr. Nau stood back, folded his arms, and let "this" sink in. I had to admit, as I examined states the size of Nevada and Texas, I was humbled. My previous lessons in American history had been a Dixiefied version of Ptolemy. My eighth-grade teacher, a pastor with more than a passing resemblance to Ronald Reagan, had dedicated his oratory skills and missionary zeal to the Battle of Shiloh. We spent an entire year on the Battle of Shiloh, culminating in a spring field trip to the sacred grounds, during which, it was rumored, Beau Graydon fingered Leanne Wilcox on the bus.

Mr. Nau's map had different ideas about American history. And as for New England, the focus of our fall semester, those "states" looked like gnats on a buffalo hide. Mr. Nau paced away, and then back to the words on the board, this time stabbing them with white chalk marks in rapid fire.

"What you've got to remember, is that it was *all about the land*. They were farmers. They were journalists. They were women and children. They went in wagons, on horses, by stagecoach. If need be they *walked*. They covered the *terrain—land*—that would be Oregon, Kansas, Nebraska. It was their *mission* to populate this country."

"Manifest. *Evident*. Destiny. *Fate*. These *pioneers* thought Divine Providence had presented the United States with a *mandate* to spread Republican democracy to what they deemed savage lands. There was a higher law at stake! Virtue. Mission. *God*. James Polk used these ideals to launch his 1844 election, feeding on the desires of a populace hungry for *land*. The resources and the crops mined from *this land* propelled this country into an economic prosperity that would make the United States the dominant *world power* it is today."

Our facial expressions had all the vibrancy of hardtack, but Mr. Nau had taken off in his own prairie schooner, consumed by the grandeur of the American West. A goner.

"The *land*, people. The *land* was why politicians waged war against Mexico and transplanted Native peoples to far corners of the desert. Today, when Caucasian descendants of Germany and Ireland and Sweden take their families for *picnics* on the *Puget Sound*, they spread their blankets on the green with *impunity*. This family named *Schmidt* or *McCormick* or *Hanson* thinks it's their right to *snack* on the former sacred *hunting grounds* of native peoples. These families drink *Coca-Colas* and eat *potato chips*. Who knows? Maybe they go *sailing* or rent a *Jet Ski*!"

That's when I saw Jon Macy's hand twitching. He was ready to ask his usual—would-this-be-on-the-test?—but when he made his move, Mr. Nau shot him down with a withering stare. Jon's hand slunk back into his lap, the clear loser in this showdown at noon.

"What you've got to remember, *people*, is that it was *all about the land*."

We allowed nothing but the barest corners of our eyeballs to reach for the clock. It was almost time for lunch.

"Land," Mr. Nau purred *sotto voce*. "Land," he said again, a bit louder, more territorial. "Land!" He growled and pointed the chalk at Jon Macy, privileged son of the wealthy who proved daily there is such a thing as a stupid question. *"Land!"* Mr. Nau accused the room, foam gathering in the corner of his mouth, his spittle daring us.

Then Jon Macy had to do it.

"What, Mr. Nau?" he said, feigning innocence. "What did you say?"

"LAND!" shouted Mr. Nau, all vestiges of polite society dissolved. His white horse teeth gleamed in the fluorescent light, armpit stains spreading like the Louisiana Purchase. He beat the map now as if slapping a mule's haunches with rawhide.

"LAND! LAND! LAND!"

Jon Macy's jaw dropped before he started laughing so hard he seized and fell, knees locked, to the floor. The bell rang, and we hurtled for the cafeteria, leaping over his corpse in our fevered desire for Tater Tots.

All our essays for that chapter read:
land land land land land
land land land land land
land land land land land
land land land land land
land land land land land
land land land land land.

Mr. Nau had provided our eleventh-grade class, one divided by southern cliques rigid as any caste system, with a story that united us all. This tale would be repeated in the halls, during class, at pep rallies, and at dances, whenever awkward teenagers needed a catch phrase to propel the conversation—which was always. Mr. Nau gave us a way to communicate in our yearbooks, something to say when the person you had known for eighteen years remained a stranger.

Ha ha, we all wrote, and we'll never forget the LAND!
The End

I drove.

The Great Plains seem incapable of modest alternations, change is always epic. The Great Plains have been desert. They have been underwater. They have been pulverized by giant sheets of ice. They have been vast prairie. They have been covered in bison and removed of bison. They have been the Dust Bowl and the Breadbasket of the World. Right now, from what I could see, the Great Plains was a vast, never-ending farmscape.

I witnessed acres upon acres of crops. I drove interstates and two-lane highways. I turned off random country roads and traced downtown grid after downtown grid. I tracked and backtracked parallel roads, bouncing back and forth around the middle of America as though I were trapped in a giant, agricultural-themed pinball machine. As Mr. Turtle and I passed miles upon hundreds of miles of cornfields,

I couldn't help but notice, *Manifest Destiny—looks like we did it.* American farmers would harvest three hundred million tons of corn from ninety-three million acres of land that year.

In simpler terms, the corn blew my mind.

From my adult's perspective, Manifest Destiny resembled the schizophrenic's alibi—"God told me to do it." We all know now that our government's invasion of the North American continent was not an act of Divine Providence, but an epic land grab. This is not to say I never saw the attraction. In Mr. Nau's class, I loved monitoring each acquisition on the map. Each time a familiar chunk of the puzzle filled in, I felt a deep satisfaction. We were the good guys, doing our job, forging America.

From Pa's perspective, pioneering wasn't just farming, but fulfilling a moral imperative. His was a time of progress, when people believed that a pure work ethic guaranteed financial reward. Americans were a deserving people, a righteous people, living during a miraculous era when any man could make his start on this rich, free land!

Sort of.

My research revealed that the Homestead Act was not such a grand gesture of our country's wealth and generosity. For one, the North wanted to populate the West with their farmers to stop the spread of slavery. President Lincoln signed the act during the Civil War, when the South no longer had a vote. Railroads also had a financial motivation; they worked with politicians who made promises about the bountiful climate. With a little convincing from the railroads, the U.S. Geological Service professed as scientific fact that "rain followed the plow." The science behind this theory was that "deep cultivation" caused water conservation. The Santa Fe Railway even proclaimed a "rainline" that ran eighteen miles ahead of settled territory.

In truth, there was good reason that the Great Plains remained the last of the U.S. territories to be farmed. I had always thought of Pa on the cusp of Westward Expansion, but most people had skipped over that arid, rugged climate in favor of the verdant Pacific Northwest or temperate California. Laura's little towns have, for the most part, remained little. De Smet's latest census put the population at 1,164—the number of people in my freshman dorm. I believe that's why it never occurred to me (before I saw that first Sign on I-90) that Laura's towns were real. My entire life I'd watched East Coast cities sprawl at an alarming rate. I assumed that if Volga or De Smet weren't by now booming urban centers around the size of Chicago or Seattle, then they must be fiction.

Instead, the Dakota farming population is shrinking. With agribusiness replacing small farms over the past fifty years, almost two-thirds of rural Great Plains towns and crossroads have lost at least one-third of their people. The dwindling numbers drain the tax base, which makes the money for new programs collapse, which causes further attrition, which further drains the tax base.

By way of response, many politicians elected from rural areas support a program that offers potential state residents "willing to commit to live and work in high out-migration rural areas for at least five years a number of financial incentives to help them buy a home, pay for college, and build savings."

This program is called the New Homestead Act.

I drove.

I passed innumerable billboards asking me if I was pregnant and wanted help. I was well past the danger of a teenage pregnancy, but neither had I experienced menopause. These constant reminders of my womb stressed me out. I was, as we might recall, raised Roman Catholic.

So, remember when My Manly and I broke up before the trip? That story had a twist I left out.

Right before that, I had experienced a late period.

I looked on the calendar and my heart jerked, and I seemed to feel it falling far, far down.

Life is all bareback pony rides across the prairie until a girl doesn't get her period.

I writhed in a state of private misery for a few weeks before I came clean to My Manly. My lack of desire for children had remained fundamentally unchanged from my teens, despite everyone's predictions to the contrary. Except now the situation was complicating—my biological window was closing. What if this was my last chance? It had been easy to know I didn't want children when I could always put off the decision until later.

Later had just turned into now.

The debate turned out to be moot. After a few sweaty moments in the bathroom, my hand shaking so hard I could barely pee on the stick, the test result showed negative. Exhale. My Manly and I were off the hook, but our relationship had quantum leaped beyond Chinese takeout and *Buffy the Vampire Slayer*. He panicked and bailed. We reunited before I left, but our future remained tentative. I had a stuffed turtle and someone to call at night, but my unspoken fear was that My Manly and I were on the big buggy ride to nowhere.

I drove.

My research continued to reveal more thorns in the sagebrush. Pa might have been an excellent carpenter, butcher, railroad worker, storyteller and musician, but he was never much of a farmer. The bumper wheat crop that would make the family rich never happened. It wasn't Pa's fault. The Dakotas are too dry. Pa was always rejoicing the lack of pesky tree roots, but there were no pesky tree roots because there were no trees, because there was no water. The 1880 census listed Pa's occupation as "carpenter," and in the end, that profession remained his mainstay. Pa sold the Dakota homestead and moved in town, where carpentry paid the bills.

The Dakota Boom was short-lived. A few years of steady rainfall seemed to support the U.S. Geological Service's claim of plow-induced precipitation, but soon after, the Plains reverted to their normal arid state. The resulting "drought" is what drove Laura and Almanzo from South Dakota to Missouri. By the time they left, 30 percent of the population had bailed on the Dakota dream. The year 1893 marked a depression era, and by 1894 one in five Americans was unemployed. In *On the Way Home*, Laura periodically catalogs farming statistics as she travels south, detailing the price of hay per ton, land per acre, wheat per bushel. Laura is worried, I can tell. She was hoping Missouri might have a more hospitable climate, but she was once more gambling her life on a place sight unseen, based on promises by a government proven to peddle untruths.

Some nineteenth-century farmers (with a little Geritol, morning walks and a daily crossword) lived to see the Homestead Act of 1862 dream realized. The historical turn here didn't take place until World War I, when the Turkish Navy blocked Russia's ability to export wheat. Capitalizing on this opportunity, the Great Plains went into wheat overdrive. Every remaining corner of virgin sod was turned over. The price of wheat rose from $1 a bushel in 1914, to $2.10 a bushel in 1917. Pa, if he had farmed forty years later, could have bought a house with store-bought panes of glass and bolts of pretty fabric for Ma.

Perhaps, that is, if Pa had remained in Kansas. Yet another flaw in the Homestead Act was that 160 acres is not enough property for a Dakota farm to turn a profit. With such low yield, vast farms are necessary, as is giant machinery that can cover the distance. When I drove across the Dakotas, I saw combines big as houses. Of the pioneers, Russian immigrant farmers fared the best, since the Great Plains resembled the Steppes of their former country. Russian farmers who could amass land from other farmers who failed did the best of all.

With the end of World War I, wheat profits dried up. From there the situation grew worse. Cycles of drought are to be expected in the farming life, but when the land went dry again in the 1930s, all the natural grasses that anchor the soil and trap water were gone. Deep plowing had not cultivated rain, but destroyed the ecosystem. Result: the Dust Bowl. Great storm clouds of dust blasted over the Plains, creating six-foot drifts along houses. Ian Frazier in *Great Plains* writes about how dust piled so high it covered fences, and livestock wandered off. It's purported that Woody Guthrie saw one of these storms headed for him and wrote his song "So Long, It's Been Good to Know You."

Eventually the drought settled out and everyone's lungs cleared out. World War II created another demand scenario, except only the wealthy with acreage and resources could capitalize. The turnaround for the average Pa would not arrive until the invention of the deep-well turbine pump. This meant farmers could tap the Ogallala Aquifer, an enormous underground water reservoir that spans from southern South Dakota (though it doesn't reach De Smet) to Texas. The Ogallala Aquifer yields 30 percent of our country's groundwater used in irrigation today.

This aquifer threatens to drain out in thirty years.

Herein lies the problem with busting historical sod. I had taken the simple pleasure of Pa whistling as he plows and unearthed economic ruin and ecological disaster.

I drove.

Around Topeka, I heard a gurgle from below. My steady fast-food diet, in addition to plaguing my waistline, had done my digestive health no favors. I had spent the previous night in Lincoln, Nebraska, and here I took full advantage of my one night in a college town by dining at an Indian restaurant where I ate pakoras, palak paneer, vegetable korma and garlic naan.

All of it.

My body, adjusted to meals of blandly spiced fat and white flour, was not pleased.

As in, it wasn't pleased *now*.

And I didn't even like to pee in the dress.

I gunned the gas and peeled off at the next exit. This was a battlefield decision driven by instinct, no time for repose. I scanned my options with a furtive eye.

Phillips 66? No, gas station bathrooms are yucky and involve keys attached to a longboat oar. McDonald's? Better, but a mother might blockade the stall as she wrestled with her toddler over who got to flush. Cracker Barrel? The bathroom would be easily located back and center of the Country Store, but I couldn't stand false-front wholesomeness right now, or the inevitable crowd.

In the clutch, my instinct told me that an all-woman staff, likewise trimmed in a humiliating shade of orange, would take me in.

Hooters it was.

Lady travelers take note: Hooters was the perfect pit stop. Hooters had few female customers, so the bathroom was empty. As purveyors of suburban soft porn, the establishment is obliged to maintain squeaky clean facilities—the metal doors and fixtures gleamed like surgical instruments. A TV had been installed in the upper right-hand corner for my amusement. A surround sound stereo thoughtfully pulsed "Maneater" by Hall and Oates, followed by "Tequila Sunrise" and "Cheeseburger in Paradise."

Often if a traveler uses the toilet with no pretense of purchase, one incurs "the eye." Not here. The Lycra-clad staff was too busy flipping through their thick wads of cash to even glance in my direction. Male customers stared a bit. Perhaps they thought I was the Hooter's madam, come down from the upstairs office to check on her girls. I ignored them and split. No Nearly World Famous Three Mile Island Chicken Wings for me, thanks.

I was exhausted, but lingering in the parking lot only meant it was that much longer until I reached my hotel, so I prodded myself to keep driving. For the first time since I left Montana, I began counting miles in my head, calculating how much more I had to go. I had zigged and zagged over the map so much I was lost, not directionally (again, it's hard to get lost on the grid), but my center was shot. I didn't know who I was anymore, where I had come from or who I was trying to be.

I drove.

I slept that night at a roadside Days Inn, my drab highway hotel room a punishment. No cozying up in pink and blue double ring wedding quilts here. I pulled back the rubbery, dubiously sanitary bedspread with a pen and sat on the threadbare sheets, feeling either hot and stuffy or frozen if I turned on the window unit. Nights like this the no-TV rule really blew. My Manly hadn't called for a few days. I worried he had received a mental transmission of my prairie wedding fantasy, thereby triggering a relapse of Male Commitment Freak-Out Syndrome. Like a Nebraska highway, my heart stretched before me, long and empty. I could call, but I didn't want to call. I wanted him to call.

I drank seltzer water for dinner and returned to *Ghost in the Little House*. I was already on my way down the bummer trail—might as well follow on through to the end. I opened the gray book with the picture of a gray woman on the cover.

Rose Wilder Lane's strong personality didn't take long to reemerge. She was too smart for her own good and stubborn from an early age. There was a story of a childhood picture for which she had insisted on wearing a ring, despite everyone's protests. While growing up, her precocious vocabulary (a product of her avid reading habit) set her apart. Haunted by her childhood in a southern town where she never quite belonged, Rose escaped the first chance she had to embark on an adulthood that was by turns adventuresome and problematic. In her journals, she ruminated for pages and pages on end about how she needed to get herself together, successes and failures tumbling over one another as she kept reinventing herself. She was a good writer, and prolific, but never quite achieved the greatness at her craft she desired. When avoiding work, she threw herself into ambitious home renovation projects. She was fiercely loyal to her friends, maintaining contacts over the years through long, heartfelt, articulate letters but was unlucky in romantic love. By middle age, plagued by bad teeth, headaches and depression, she realized love had passed her by...

Rose reminded me of someone.

The angst, the drama, the internal conflicts, the stubbornness, the constant self-analysis, the resolutions, the epic to-do lists, the striking off to reinvent herself and the periodic depressions—it all felt pretty familiar—right down to the story of a childhood portrait where a kooky kid insists on clutching her talisman. I wasn't toothless and unlucky in love (yet), but I was thirty-eight, my relationship a half-stitched ostrich feather clinging to a poke bonnet. My entire life I had harbored a secret hope that I was reincarnation of Laura Ingalls Wilder. Given this new information, it seemed much more likely I was her daughter. Rose had died in October of 1968, the same month of my birth. What more proof did I need?

I wished that the title of Holtz's book had been *Rose Wilder Lane: Awesome if Somewhat Flawed in a Loveable Way*, but no, *Ghost in the Little House* was as much about tearing Laura down as it was profiling the tortured daughter. My initial fears were confirmed as Professor Killjoy went on to proclaim that Laura was some kind of *Country*

Living mommy dearest, an overbearing matriarch who "ruled the family with an iron fist." And stingy! Mercy, did Holtz portray Laura as miserly, a woman who pinched pennies with the grip of a practiced milker. An extension of Laura's abuse was that she turned her daughter into her authorial slave.

Then Holtz got into the psychoanalysis.

Quoting Alice Miller, author of *The Drama of the Gifted Child*, Holtz wrote about how intelligent, sensitive children can be damaged by parents who control them with overly rigid, adult standards of behavior. The result is that these children can only see themselves as instruments of the parents' vision, and thus never feel able to authenticate their own desires. Robbed of their childhood, they grow up with emptiness at the core of their being.

"Gifted" was how educators in my public school system described kids with above-average IQs. I had been identified "gifted" in third grade, and my failure to succeed as an astronaut/ballerina had weighed upon me ever since.

"You know," my mother has always been fond of saying, "you've been tested, and you can do anything you want." (Read: Doctor.)

My parents, both Ed.Ds, had a copy of *The Drama of the Gifted Child* on our bookshelf next to *Shogun* and *The Naked and the Dead*. I remember when I first saw the red paperback with white print running down the spine. *Yes!* I thought. *This book will explain away my angst, and then I can fix myself.* But *The Drama of the Gifted Child* only contributed to my drama, because I couldn't get through Miller's book, which made me feel ungifted. (*The Naked and the Dead* and *Shogun* left me similarly bereft.) Now that Holtz had provided me with the Spark Notes version, I had to wonder if there was something to the Miller/Holtz argument. Maybe my adult indecisiveness and anxieties weren't rooted in a lack of childhood farm chores, but my strictly tracked childhood. Rose had certainly grown up with plenty of stalls to muck, but her letters and journals prove that whatever her successes—traipsing the globe, publishing in glossy magazines or building dream homes—she more often felt like a failure and would torture herself over the least little problem.

I refreshed my glass of club soda and tried to ignore the aroma of industrial laundry detergent and musty carpet. Even with the vinyl blinds drawn tight, the invasive fluorescent light from the parking lot bore through. The more I probed, the more my discoveries went viral, replicating beyond my control. I resolved to set aside the psychoanalysis. First and foremost was the question of authorship, around which all these other identity issues hinged.

I had biographies of Laura and Rose that offered alternate points of view. I also had *Young Pioneers* and *Free Land*, Rose's pioneer novels, as well as letters and writings that were indisputably Laura's. If I read these materials and compared them to the Books, I felt confident I would know the truth. What this all had to do with me and my quest would simply have to sort itself out. For now, I absorbed myself in research.

CHAPTER TWELVE
HOMECOMING

Mansfield, Missouri

Before this trip, the South had always been my starting point. It was strange to begin north and travel down, and stranger still that the farther I drove, the more familiar the landscape became. Southeastern Kansas is technically the Midwest, but there's a twang around the edges. Further east, moving into Missouri, the Ozark foothills rose. The climate turned warm and damp, leafy green trees and earthen smells contributing to a spooky sense of déjà vu. Churches morphed from little white Lutheran houses into brick Baptist stadiums. Local businesses got personal: Joe's Vacuum Repair, Katie's Kwik Kurl, Dusty Doug's Body Shop. The number of RV parks and gun and pawn shops per capita increased. Kudzu snarled over dead cars, scrap metal sculptures and baby pools. The sky grew close. Animals, children and flowers were everywhere.

At my next meal I gave the test.

"Sweet tea?" I asked.

"Cornbread or rolls?" replied the waiter, not skipping a beat.

A few minutes later my plate of fried catfish, collards and squash casserole arrived.

I was back.

I have always loved southern food, southern flowers and southern skies, but politically and socially speaking, my life in the South has traditionally been a troubled fit. My parents are from Buffalo and for a long time, my accent showed it. I wasn't country enough for my public junior high and wasn't country club enough for my private high school. I have previously detailed my failure at southern hair. I could, possibly, have survived these estrangements except for this deal breaker (whispering): *I don't care about football.* Tuscaloosans erect marble statues of Paul Bear Bryant in their foyers and tattoo their bodies houndstooth. I would go shopping fall Saturdays and wonder why Tuscaloosa resembled the apocalypse (no signs of life, the same radio broadcast all over town) before I remembered—*Oh.* I am nervous to publicly admit my apathy toward the state obsession. In Crimson Tide country, disloyalty to "the program" is grounds for excommunication followed by skinning alive concluded by a thorough grave trampling. My lack of interest ranks me below an Auburn fan, and trust me, that is very, very low.

Bottom line: I never belonged. My entire childhood seemed as though some spaceship had plunked me down and split for planets unknown. I moved to Alabama as an infant, lived there for eighteen years, and continued to live in the South for nineteen years after that, yet when I go to visit my parents, strangers halt midconversation to interject, "You're not from around here, are ya?" So, as the foliage grew lush and the home-cooking increasingly delicious, my nerves began to fray. I was returning to the people who had never embraced me—now in a big, flowered prairie dress. Was this my desperate, last-ditch audition for Azalea Trail Maid? I had adjusted to my role in the rural Midwest as the politely acknowledged outsider, but southerners are not poker-faced Lutherans. Southerners are an intense people, with intense emotions and strong opinions. I would know what they thought.

Meanwhile, I was about ready to rip off this dress and dispose of it like a garment from a crime scene. It wasn't made for daily wear and my rib cage yearned for freedom. The zipper dance was old, and my hair kept twisting in the metal teeth; there was a permanent little rat's nest in the middle. I was sick of kicking the flounce around as I hit the gas and braked. The bonnet strings choked my neck, and the cap sleeves pinched my arms. I craved my faded jeans and tank top. The Kelly Kathleen Ferguson rationalization machine cranked into overdrive. I had worn the dress through De Smet, which heralded the end of the Books. That was enough, right? Really, what was the point in wowing a few more gas station cashiers? Besides, I would drive most of the day only to reach Mansfield and spend a few hours there before I turned and drove right back out. It seemed completely reasonable that I deserved to experience Mansfield as a regular tourist, where I could walk around in blissful anonymity.

I was struck by the egotism of my quest. It wasn't as if I were some pioneer superhero, swooping upon the plains to help beleaguered homesteaders with their chores. There was no one who cared about this dress or this trip but me. I was tired of being stared at. I was tired of the questions. I was tired of Lutherans *not* asking questions. I was tired of feeling like a weirdo, a label that had haunted me since third grade, the day Julie Anne Crawford poked my arm while I was peacefully coloring and demanded to know, "Why are you so weird?"

Weird had never been my intention. No, I wanted to be tiny and adored with Farrah Fawcett–feathered hair, like Julie Anne Crawford.

There was no denying it, this last stop had taken on the gray flavor of a chore. I wanted to feel excitement as I rounded the bend for my final lap, but I was an evacuated shell like the fish skull from Lake Pepin. I retreated into a familiar, blank state of southern malaise, shutting down, spacing out.

Part of why my re-coming of age on this trip had felt so immediate was that much of the rural Great Plains remained circa 1970s. Bank signs, gas pumps, telephone poles and traffic lights (the yellow kind) would take me back in sudden flashes to my childhood. These were the artifacts I didn't realize I had forgotten until I saw them again. In Walnut Grove, there was a Superman telephone booth. It no longer had the telephone, but I slid open the glass door and leaned against the glass wall, remembering how I used to scramble for dimes, the texture of the metal rattail cord, the fury over consumed change and monotone operators. The ghost sound of a dial tone rang in my ear.

I had cruised through Mankato and Topeka, but those cities still felt remote—a blip of industry and good-bye. It wasn't until Springfield, Missouri, that I experienced a jolting reentry into the twenty-first-century world of billboards, four-lane highways, barreling eighteen-wheelers and perpetual roadside construction. With the increased pace and population, my snake brain emerged from hibernation, wary of potential danger. An undercurrent of modern anxiety began to percolate beneath my state of depressed exhaustion. I gripped the steering wheel and weaved through traffic.

Which is not to say urban sprawl is without its advantages. I took an exit so I could grab some twenty-first-century solace in the form of a Starbucks coffee. People claim Starbucks is taking over the world, but I'm here to testify that miles and miles and miles of this country have no Starbucks and that the roadside traveler must drink reduction sludge salvaged from the bottom of convenience store coffee pots. It was surreal to hold a fresh, foamy latte again, and a little hypocritical. Here I had been waxing lyrical about the power of rustic pioneer life, only to find myself sitting in a strip mall parking lot gently caressing a Venti Dulce de Leche.

I sipped and braced myself for the final regroup in my metal cell. By this point the car was trashed: crumpled fast-food bags, dirty laundry, straw wrappers, receipts, soda bottles, hair scrunchies and Humpty-Dumptied books on tape that would soon terminate my relationship with the Missoula Public Library. The upholstery reeked of fryer grease and human desperation. My inner spirit candle was burnt to a nub, and My Manly's disappearing act getting to me more than I cared to admit. A heaviness set that I couldn't shake. In theory retail chains seek to comfort in their consistency, but for me they create an aura of nowheresville. I could have been in Alabama, North Carolina, Montana, Minnesota or the Aleutian Islands. There was absolutely nothing unique about my surroundings, giving me the unsettling suspicion that I had made no progress at all.

In search of comfort, I turned and reached for my standby in the backseat, the map, and, hey, while I was turned around, I might as well grab that donut I had purposefully placed beyond temptation's reach—a mistake. With that extra stretch came a tearing sound, *rrrrrrrriffft*. My dress split at the waist and a well of white belly fat plopped out. Mortified, I froze for a moment in denial and then, I am ashamed to report, two big tears welled up in each eye before the levees broke and I boohooed facedown on the wheel. Sensing opportunity, my old mental misery tape cranked back into gear. *I'm alone. All alone. Why am I always all alone?*

"For shame!" I could hear Ma scolding in the back of my head. "A big girl like you. For shame!" Laura was too old to cry by the age of three, and I was a bit older than that. I was regressing. This is what going home does to a person. I was right back at personal growth ground zero, the girl with self-esteem the texture of grape jelly.

I needed support. I needed the friend you call at 3 a.m. after you upturned a bucket of bourbon, went to a karaoke bar, tearfully dedicated Lionel Richie's "Lady" to your dead dog, staggered offstage, hit on every man/woman/machine in the room before puking in the backseat of your unrequited crush's car who is driving you home only so he can hook up with your better-looking housemate. This is the friend you dial sputtering *wob wob wob* and she says *I know.* The friend you summon after you have been driving for days and days in a prairie dress one-quarter size too small and you don't really know why and she doesn't really either, but she loves you for whatever it is you need loving for.

"Annnnaaaaaaaaaa," I wailed. "I don't wanna wear this dress anymore. It ripped and my fat spilled out."

"Oh, Kelly. You are not fat."

"*Whine. Whine. Whine. Whine. Whine.* And furthermore, *Wah*," I said.

"You are so close! I'm counting on you."

"My Manly hasn't called."

"Oh," said Anna.

"I know," I said.

"You could just wear the bonnet."

"No," I sniffled. "That's no good."

"I know," she said.

Sometimes all you need is one person in the world holding you accountable. After all, Laura buckled down and earned her teacher's certificate for Mary, not for herself. Revived, I tucked in some fabric to cover my exposed skin and started the car—time to enter the belly of the corn-fed beast. As a consolation, I decided I didn't have to kid myself about trying to interact with people anymore. No more playing around as a guerilla tour guide or forced small talk with cashiers in need of job counseling. I would don my "don't talk to me" mask (perfected from years of afternoon bartending), go in, do my tour and get on with my life. Given the world's inclination to ignore me, my plan should execute without a hiccup.

It could have been the espresso, or perhaps I was stir-crazy after hours in a car, but after days of languid lolling over rural roads followed by a depressed state followed by an anxious yet depressed state, a frantic energy took over. I began speeding for the first time since that ticket in South Dakota. Past the bustle of Springfield, the highway grew rural again, and I hit cruising altitude. All my nervous prickles focused into a pinpoint: Destination, Mansfield.

Within an hour a Sign of enormous proportions came into view: a billboard proclaiming *See the Laura Ingalls Wilder Historic Home Turn Here*, with a mammoth arrow pointing right. In Laura's last diary entry, she describes Mansfield as a town of about 350. She mourns the lack of a Congregational church and lists the businesses (two general stores, two drug stores, the bank, a Boston Racket store, livery stable, blacksmith shop). Her last sentence mentions that Manly is checking out a property, and that's all Laura writes for a long time. It took the Wilders a while to find the right place, and when they did—signing the paperwork on Rocky Ridge Farm September 21, 1894—she had to put down her pencil and dedicate both hands to clearing, building and planting.

The twenty-first-century Mansfield downtown consisted of a few insurance offices, some empty storefronts, a Chinese restaurant and a bank. I meandered down the tree-lined country road that led to the last homesite, rattled into the gravel parking and threw the Camry into park. Mansfield also has a Memorial Society active in the preservation of Laura history. This site is considered the hub because it has the largest museum housing the greatest number of artifacts. Laura and Almanzo's white clapboard house and the visitor's center were up on a grassy hill covered in lawn and trees. It didn't seem to be an especially big day, but business was steady.

I kicked open the car door and walked up the hill in one fluid motion, no hesitation in my stride, but with all the excitement of a patient headed to the immunization clinic.

A small army of elderly Lauras populated the homesite; short, white-haired, bright-eyed women in prairie dresses. They were everywhere—standing in doorways, giving tours and projecting educational films. Inside the museum entrance, behind the ticket counter, one of these Ozark golden girls put down her needlework to take my money. The apron covered most of my dress tear, but I could feel the air on my skin. I pulled a few greasy, crumpled bills from my bag, avoiding eye contact.

"Why, look at you!" the Laura said with a broad smile.

I didn't mean to be rude, but I stood there, mouth agape, unable to respond. A person had *initiated* conversation with me. I suppose I had grown so inured to being ignored I didn't expect anyone to comment anymore. Why, it had been so long I teared up again, still a little weepy from my earlier breakdown.

"That is such a pretty dress!" she exclaimed.

I could barely speak, but my training kicked in and I choked out, "Thank you, ma'am."

"Did you make it yourself?" she asked.

"Oh, no. And I bought the bonnet and apron."

"Well, isn't that wonderful! I hope you enjoy your visit."

It was as though my invisibility potion had worn off. Everywhere I went people stopped to comment and compliment me.

"Why, isn't that a pretty dress!" most of them said.

"Don't ever grow up!" said a mother of two. "Stay young at heart forever!"

"Are you Alice in Wonderland?" asked a woman.

The visitor's center features a substantial museum, and Mansfield has the most artifacts of any site. Pa's fiddle is on display along with Ma's pearl-handled pen and Mary's Braille slate. There were quilts, china, furniture and even the Ingalls family Bible. Rose had a substantial corner devoted to her, containing possessions and pictures, as well as her handiwork—both domestic and literary.

159

Laura's original jewel box with the little teacup and saucer was there, but chipped. A bit nervous now, I checked for the china shepherdess, but she was nowhere to be found. I asked, and the shepherdess, apparently, is MIA. To my mind this was much better than cracked and on display. My travel-worn psyche couldn't withstand the disaster of a chipped china shepherdess. I prefer she continue to live intact forever in my mind, still emerging from the box at every destination unflawed.

A profile of Laura the industrious country farmwoman with the complicated daughter was beginning to come together. There had been, after all, forty-seven years of life that fell between her wedding day and the writing of her first book, and here were the artifacts to prove it, not to mention the farmland surrounding the museum. Evidences of Laura's late-life career as a renowned author were also on display. A back wall displayed book editions from around the world.

Before I left, I stared at a photo of Laura in her late sixties, the age she was writing and publishing the Books. I was stunned by how pretty she was, the bright, white hair pulled back in a bun, the sparkle in her eyes. In a flash of knowing I thought *yes*, that's exactly how I want to be at that age.

Another Laura took us on the tour of the Wilder home. In 1896, the Wilders built the first frame room of what would become the white house on the hill. From 1911–1913 they built additions until their home was complete—nine rooms in all. The house has been preserved since Laura and Almanzo lived there, with all the knickknacks, toiletries and kitchen utensils still in place.

Just as Pa had done for Ma, Almanzo custom built the kitchen cabinets for Laura, keeping her five-foot frame in mind. Maybe I was Alice in Wonderland after all, when she ate the cake and grew to nine feet tall. The canary yellow room, even after all the years gone by and restorations, struck me as a place of industry. The eggbeater, potholders and crockery were all handy and ready to go. If I hadn't already been in an apron, I would have wanted to put one on. These days a "country kitchen" look means blue geese and pink hearts, but this was the real deal. Here was a place to can, preserve, churn and roll out biscuits.

As we explored room by room, the inevitable happened—I fell in love. I loved the colors that were a little too bright and the sturdy antique furniture. I loved the wood beamed ceiling and the rocking chairs and the fireplace and the little library off the parlor. Laura, who was born the same year as Frank Lloyd Wright, shared the architect's view that a house should complement the land, insisting the house be built of natural materials from the property, such as oak and stone. I loved that, too. Past the kitchen were forbidden stairs (always forbidden, these historic stairs!) that once led to Rose's childhood sleeping loft. I wanted to crawl up there and take a nap. Forever. If asked, I would have gone out to the car, gotten my suitcase, and moved right in, leaving everything else I ever owned behind.

Fortunately for Laura and Almanzo, Mansfield is good farming country, although it took around twenty years to get the place running. Rocks had to be hauled and trees cleared. The farm came with several hundred apple tree seedlings—all unplanted. Laura's outdoor skills continued to be useful; she explained to a reporter once that her husband would rather have her on the other end of a crosscut saw than any man. Almanzo's specialty became Jersey cows while Laura worked the Leghorn poultry angle. Through the years they established the orchards of apples and pears they could have never grown in the Dakotas. Laura and Manly were also social in town, active in religious and charitable organizations, such as their Methodist Church and the Eastern Star.

In sum, Laura and Almanzo shared an entire life together, keeping their promise for sixty-four years. There is an iconic photo of them standing companionably side by side before their farmhouse. Manly has an adorable white moustache and wears suspenders. Laura looks like the Hallmark greeting card grandmother. When Almanzo died, Laura slept in his twin bed until she passed ten years later. She could never bring herself to throw away his toiletries. Almanzo's Vick's rub, eye-drops, cod-liver oil and Listerine all remain to this day in his medicine box.

I thought of my one, cautiously placed toothbrush at My Manly's. Before we were asked to exit, I ran back for one last look at my favorite part. Adjoining the bedroom was Laura's little writing study. Laura's adult writing career began at forty-four, when she wrote a speech for a friend and the editor of the *Missouri Ruralist*, impressed by Laura's prose, offered her a column. Laura went on to write "As a Farm Woman Thinks" from 1911 to 1924 and eventually took on other articles for payment. From there, her ambitions turned from journalism to storytelling, although it would be another twenty years before her first book.

The modest secretary's desk sat against the flowered wall. Little cubbies held pencils and Laura's famous orange-covered notebooks on which she wrote the Books. Laura started a whole new life as an author at sixty-five, publishing her first book, *Little House in the Big Woods*, in 1932. I imagined Laura waking up in the middle of the night, running over to capture a few words. There was a "fainting couch" near the desk, so named for when women passed out from wearing their tight corsets. Sometimes Almanzo would wake up to find Laura asleep there, exhausted from writing.

Somehow I had always known that Laura was a literary late bloomer. Through my high school, college and restaurant years I hoarded this fact like a stashed gold nugget, this idea that it's never too late. Teaching was the cardigan that fit, but what I had been waiting for all those years was to be a writer. Throughout my twenties the very word *writer* was an ice pick to my chest. What kept me going through the endless bus tubs and service trays was this idea that, like Laura, I would one day publish books. Furthermore, these books would reflect the experience of a writer who had lived, who had lived a life worth writing about. Laura lived first and wrote later.

I can only imagine what determination it took to write those books after decades of farming. The Laura who showed Nellie who was boss, who beat Mrs. White making buttonholes, who hauled a cord of wood one Minnesota blizzard—that's the Laura who decided she could publish, too. For this final goal of mine, I hoped to draw upon Laura's strength one more time.

Down the road from the farmhouse was the Rock House, which Rose had built in 1928, when she returned to her childhood home after one of her adventurous sojourns, this time in Albania. It's hard to say if Rose returned to Missouri because her Albania dreams went belly up (for years her plan had been to stay there), or if her parents needed her, or if she *wanted* her parents to need her and she took on the role of martyr. When there's drama of the gifted child involved, the situation is always complicated.

Rose left Mansfield at seventeen for Kansas City, to work as a telegraph operator for three years. From there she moved to San Francisco where she first broke into writing. Rose was an established author long before her mother, her articles and short stories appearing in such mainstays as the *Saturday Evening Post, Gentlemen's Quarterly, Harper's* and *Good Housekeeping*. She wrote seventeen books, ranging from biographies of Henry Ford and Charlie Chaplin to fiction novels about frontier life (material she plucked from her mother). A contemporary of such luminaries as Sherwood Anderson and Upton Sinclair, many of Rose's publications were on display in the museum. Her bibliography was impressive.

In San Francisco, Rose met and married Gillette Lane, although the couple eventually divorced in 1918. Single once more, these were years of extensive worldwide travel for Rose, her work taking her to such locations as New York, Paris, Athens, Budapest and Vienna. I don't imagine she ever expected to live in Missouri again, but then she returned at the age of forty. With her typical maniacal drive, Rose threw her energies into the designing of the Rock House,

The tan, brown and gray fieldstone house looked as though it had been airlifted from Staffordshire and placed back down in Missouri, although the plans were, in fact, ordered from Sears and Roebuck. A guide was there but there wasn't much to show, as the interior was unfurnished. The house was remarkably up to date, more 1970s than 1920s, looking the way some people design their houses retro on purpose. The tiny, square aqua-tiles of the bathroom especially took me back.

In 1928, Rose unveiled the house to her parents as a gift and moved herself into the white clapboard farmhouse. It was in the Rock House that Laura would eventually write her first four published books. Laura's first attempt at a novel-length work was the memoir *Pioneer Girl*, which condensed the chronology of all the

Books into one. A routine developed whereby Laura and Rose would walk the footpath between farmhouse and the Rock House and go over parts together. Rose typed Laura's handwritten manuscript up and sent it to her agent, and eventually this draft morphed into *Little House in the Big Woods*. Although released during the Depression (or I suspect, because), *Big Woods* sold well, as did *Farmer Boy* and *Little House on the Prairie*.

Laura continued to write and publish until she finished the entire series, completing *These Happy Golden Years* by the age of seventy-six. Throughout Laura's lifetime the Books continued to sell and win awards. She had libraries and wings of libraries named for her. In 1953, the box set, my box set, featuring the illustrations by Garth Williams, was released, and Laura's vision of all the Books reading as one big book was realized.

The Rock House had high ceilings, a sensible layout and all the modern conveniences, but I missed the low oak beams and sprawling charm of the farmhouse. Laura did, too. When Rose left in 1935, Laura and Almanzo moved back to their original home, and that's where they remained the rest of their days. Although sacks of fan mail distinguished Laura from the average Mansfield resident, on a day-to-day basis she continued life as usual on the farm. Almanzo puttered in his shop, and Laura fed the turtles that came to visit at her door. After Almanzo died of heart failure, friends and neighbors looked after Laura until her diabetes deteriorated to a point that Rose came for the final days. Rose, by this point, was settled in Danbury, Connecticut, where she had reinvented herself as a political activist, and is even credited with helping to found and name the Libertarian Party. In motion to the end, Rose had planned an extended sojourn to Europe and possibly the Middle East the night before her death at the age of eighty-one.

By this point I was ready to face Dr. Bummertude. I had read a few bios by now, as well as original work by Rose and Laura. My bottom line was that my initial instincts were unchanged: I wasn't buying what he was selling. I did believe that Rose's contributions were pivotal, but Pamela Smith Hill, in *Laura Ingalls Wilder: A Writer's Life*, points out that Rose's role was in line with that of an editor. Letters and revised manuscripts that Laura and Rose sent back and forth can now be viewed in the archives of the Herbert Hoover Presidential Library and Museum in Iowa. Excerpts from these correspondences are cited in both Holtz's and Hill's books. The letters demonstrate an active dialogue between writer and editor as the two struggled and debated over character development and plot points. Admittedly, Rose took her editorial responsibilities to an extreme. At times she slashed and inserted entire passages.

Could another editor have accomplished the same work as Rose? I can't imagine anyone who would have had the same personal investment, or the intimate understanding of the material. Rose was a savvy, seasoned writer and instrumental in helping Laura shape the work as well as make the necessary publishing connections. For all of that I give Rose credit. My final conclusion, though, having read Rose's original work, was that her prose fell flat. Her voice borders on melodrama, the characters are not especially compelling, and the plot points drag. Rose's insistence on conflict and inclusion of more dialogue did spice up the Books. Even so, I preferred Laura's unshaped diary entries to Rose's finished stories. The voice, the story, the descriptive passages and the core vision of the Books—I had no doubt these were born of Laura. Laura all the way.

Final thoughts: the Rose and Laura literary duo made the famous writer/editor relationship of Maxwell Perkins and F. Scott Fitzgerald look like schoolboys in a spitting contest. And as for the Laura I had grown up with, whom I knew from the Books, she was the same as always.

Which took me back to my real problem. Me.

By the time I returned to the visitor's center, the grounds had emptied out. I went to the Book and Souvenir Store to pick up a few last items. I was the only person in the room except for two Lauras working the register—I'll call them Carrie and Grace. A black and white map called "Laura's Travels" hung on the wall behind them, little dashes marking Laura's pioneer journey, and now mine. Carrie and Grace had a conversational patter going, and it took me a while to realize they were talking to me. I kept forgetting I was visible again. By this point I had finished my shopping, which consisted of a few postcards.

"I'll take one of those maps, too," I said. "I like maps."

"You know when we were growing up, Laura was nobody extraordinary. Just another farm woman," said Carrie, clacking away at her needlework.

"Just like anyone else," said Grace.

"She spoke at my school once when I was little. I really can't remember much. If I had known she was important, I would have paid more attention," said Carrie.

"That's amazing!" I said. "All I ever learned about in school was the Battle of Shiloh."

"Laura saved buttons, you know. And she loved to cook," said Grace.

"My older sister loves to cook, but not me. I hardly ever cook a thing," said Carrie.

"No, and that's all for the best."

"I can't boil water. It's a tragedy."

"Her kids have locked up the pots and pans in the pantry so she can't reach them."

"Oh it's true. So true," Carrie keened. "Every pot roast I make turns to stone."

"What you do is, take it out before you think it's done, and then it won't be so dry."

"But I can't take it pink. I have got to have it done."

"My mom made a lot of tuna fish sandwiches, and now mayo gives me a gag reflex," I said. "But she's a good person."

Carrie picked up one of my postcards. It was a profile of Laura looking around thirty, dressed to the hilt. Her head is tilted saucily in profile, all the better to display her gaudy hat with long feathers jutting out the back. The women exchanged conspiratorial glances.

"Should we tell her the ghost story?" asked Carrie.

"I think she'd appreciate it," said Grace.

"Let's do it," they said.

"Do you want to hear a ghost story?" asked Carrie.

"Sure, I—"

"Well, we were here one day talking about how we don't like that picture," began Carrie.

166

"You've got to back up or she won't understand!" said Grace.

"Oh, alright!" Carrie glanced back over her shoulder and then both ways before she continued in a low voice. "Now. For this picture Laura and Rose went to Kansas City to have portraits made. Rose— I never met her—she insisted they get all done up, but you see Laura wasn't like that. I mean, Laura did like to dress up, but in her own way. Not Rose's way. With that fussy dress and the big, draping sleeves."

"That hair!"

"See here? Her hair is all piled up on her head, and she is wearing that ridiculous hat with those feathers flying out the back. She is so primped."

"Her hip jutting out!"

"It's not really like her."

Carrie and Grace shook their heads.

"So we were here at work," said Carrie, "just like this, and we were both talking, just like this, about how we never liked that picture, and how it didn't look like her, but like something Rose made her do, and the bouffant hair and, well, everything."

Grace nodded.

"Then I said—" Carrie lowered her voice down to a whisper, "I said that she looked more like *Mrs. Oleson.*"

The women covered their mouths and doubled over laughing.

"Laura didn't care for that one bit!" gasped Carrie.

"Not one bit."

"And then, that postcard rack—"

"—The one right over there!"

"It fell over."

"The whole thing!"

"All the cards fell down—"

"—They went everywhere! Covering the floor!"

They silenced, creating a dramatic pause.

"But one card remained face up..."

"*This card.*" Grace held up my postcard.

"People don't believe us, but it's true."

"A shiver ran cold right up my spine!"

"If we didn't see it, we would have never believed it."

I scanned the room. *Laura? Are you here?*

"Now isn't that a pretty dress," said Grace. "Did you make it?"

"No, I'm afraid my sewing is about like Carrie's cooking."

"Well, it's pretty and you look very nice in it."

"I'm sick of this dress," I admitted. "I feel stupid."

"But *why?*" Carrie and Grace said.

"I mean, isn't this a little bit ridiculous? Me wearing this dress around?"

"No!" they exclaimed.

"I'm almost forty," I said.

"You just keep wearing that dress and don't you mind what other people say."

"Why, life is like Christmas Day. Over before you know it."

"But—do you think Laura would like it?" I asked.

"She would love it!"

"She always did like attention," agreed the other.

"Come to think of it," I said, examining the postcard. "That hat does look like something Mrs. Oleson would wear."

I clapped my hand over my mouth. All three of us looked warily at the postcard tree, waiting to see what Laura would do.

There's a bust of Laura in the Mansfield town square, a little patch of green with trees surrounded by a sidewalk. It sits alone, this floating head in the park, staring in perpetuity at the Mansfield Bank. Laura was fond of savings, so I imagine this vista pleases her. This was it, my final stop before I turned back around. Me and a bust and Mansfield, Missouri, which, come to think of it, sounded like an old Broadway show tune, except I was feeling less than jazzy. A Rose-like angst ping-ponged inside my chest, and the aftereffects of Starbucks coffee jittered through my bloodstream. I looked into Laura's eyes and rubbed the cold metal cheek as if conjuring a genie.

I had spent a good deal of my adult life wondering how my life might have been different, if this or if that. What if I had taken the reporter's job in Hillsborough? What if I had moved to New York after college instead of whiling away in Durham? What if I had the courage to start writing earlier? What if _____ (insert ex's name here) had been the love of my life instead of a tool? What if I hadn't wasted so much time in an existential funk? These were all valid questions, and all incredibly useless.

I couldn't say, standing here in a park with a sculpted metal head of Laura Ingalls Wilder at the end of my quest, that I had suddenly self-actualized. I remained wobbly inside. My internal structural flaws, although vastly reinforced, would probably always haunt me. But I also knew that a fear of risk would never again keep me from risking. I was no longer waiting to feel grown-up, because instead I had decided to be grown-up, the way I am, the best that I could.

No, Laura had not magically vaporized from a barn to pen these fantastic books. She worked as a columnist for years and had editorial assistance. Nor was Laura a saint. She had been an imperfect mother, and an imperfect farmer, and probably an imperfect many things. But her successes struck me as no less incredible than they ever had.

Laura and Manly, after setbacks that would break most people today, established a working farm and built an adorable house with a bright yellow kitchen where Laura baked delicious gingerbread. Through all of their difficulties, they maintained a successful partnership, by all accounts loving. Some people give up in old age. Laura invented a whole new chapter for herself as an author.

And as for Pa, no, he never turned his 160 acres into a wheat gold mine, but he did earn the deed to his land while most homesteaders packed it in. Charles Ingalls's resourcefulness and work ethic and music kept the family going. His stories shaped a daughter who became a world-famous author. On his deathbed, Pa's family rallied to be there for him, not so easy in the nineteenth century. I've known people "too busy" to drive across town to visit their parents in the hospital.

Because of Laura, who inspired my move West, and this trip, and my teaching career, and who had inspired me to write, I wouldn't have to ask myself anymore, "What if?"

It's awkward to hug a metal bust because there's no real body, but I did my best, wrapping my arms around her neck stump.

"Laura," I said. "You don't have to be perfect for me to love you. You have always admitted your flaws. That's one of the qualities I have always admired."

I planted a kiss on Laura's cool metal cheek.

A mere two hours had passed since I crossed the Mansfield city line. I drove back out the country road that had brought me in and merged back onto the highway. Facing me was the haul back to Montana. I was empty behind the eyes and my body ached, but my mind, if weary, was clear. The grunge, Gen-X chattering monkey in my mind had died and gone to heaven. As I am pretty much accustomed to a barrage of internal questioning, this quiet was odd. I let the silence hang there, observing it as if a new life form. Then, as the car gathered highway speed, a tingle sparked at the bottom of my chest before it swelled up and outward.

I had done it.

I had completed my life regression, proven myself a doer, a traveler, an accomplisher of deeds. I had persevered. I had crossed the Continental Divide and made a whole new set of friends. I had traveled alone, talked to strangers, navigated highways and byways. I had experienced exotic adventures, and in the seemingly least exotic of places.

I was feeling, as Pa would say, this was a job well done.

That night I slept in Baxter Springs, Kansas, in an old downtown office space converted into a bed and breakfast. The rooms were upstairs, and a huge hallway bisected the second story with the old doors lining each side. I was the only guest that night, and the owner gave me the mega suite, a corner room that overlooked the downtown with giant picture windows. My quarters featured a separate living room, which must have been the waiting room of a doctor or a dentist once.

My rising sign is Cancer. In *The Inner Sky*, astrologist Steven Forrest says that what is hardest for Cancers is exactly what they must do to fight stagnation—molt. I unzipped the dress and threw it on the bed. Defrocked, my new, tender, white crustacean body emerged. I

170

sat on one of the Queen Anne red velvet loveseats and stared at my crumpled shell of turquoise flowers with the traffic cone flounce, a little more wilted than when I began in Pepin. *You know,* I thought, *that is a pretty dress.*

Right then what I call the Verizon Boogie Fever ringtone broke the silence of my room. I knew who it was, just like Laura knew on Sundays who'd be coming around in a buggy for a ride. I scurried frantically for my phone, suddenly wanting like nothing else to celebrate my victory with someone else.

Five months later, that Christmas, My Manly and I unwrapped the presents under our fiber-optic tree. That evening we would have duck breasts in port wine reduction sauce with *confit de canard,* roasted fingerling potatoes, *haricot verts* and individual apple/pear crisps with vanilla ice cream. My Manly was discussing (as he had been for a while) his plans to go to Prince Edward Island and live for a year in a house his parents owned. He was stuck and moving in circles, he said, and he needed a change. Life was fine, but he wanted better than fine. If anyone understood what he was talking about, it was me, but a lump clutched in my chest.

What about me? I thought. *Am I a part of these plans? Wouldn't it be sad and boring at PEI without me?* This was the unsaid in the room, or at least it was for me. I was waiting for a gesture that I might factor in. At this point in our relationship I was pretty fluent in oyster, the micro-facial twitches and eyeball maneuvers that keyed me in to My Manly's clammed-up thoughts, but today I couldn't crack the code. Outside I'd plastered on my big Christmas smile. Inside I was a wreck. This was what happened when My Manly brought up PEI, and if I asked any questions, his oyster mode cranked into overdrive and the evening turned awkward.

My Manly handed me a heavy, rectangular present. It wasn't a tiny box, but I could tell by the look on his face that this gift was important. I pulled back a corner of wrapping paper and saw a flash of bright forest-green. On the side was an illustration of a young girl with red hair and a straw hat.

A green box set.

I pulled out *Anne of Green Gables.*

"It's not just the one book, but the *whole set*," said My Manly, his cheeks flushing pink a little.

"I know!" I said and launched into his arms.

I put the green box next to the yellow one on my shelf.

Laura Ingalls, meet Anne Shirley.

CHAPTER THIRTEEN
RECKONING

If we would win success in anything, when we come to a wall that bars our way we must throw our hearts over and then follow confidently. It is fairy advice, you know, and savors of magic, so following it we will ride with the fairies of good fortune and go safely over.

—Laura Ingalls Wilder, "As a Farmwoman Thinks"

Technically, the box set finishes with *The First Four Years*, which chronicles the somber story of Laura and Almanzo's early marriage. To my mind, this book is a childhood literary trauma trumped only by *Old Yeller*. *I'm just a kid*, I remember thinking the first (and last) time I read it. *Why are you doing this to me?* That's why when I read the Books, I always stop with *Golden Years*, and with this book, I invite you to do the same. If you prefer the romantic happy golden ending, read no further. After some debate, I have included what happened next, because to ignore this epilogue would be a disservice to my fellow humans who do not live lives scripted by the Harlequin writing staff. More importantly, I learned that Laura wasn't done with me yet.

I wish I could say that My Manly and I went to Prince Edward Island where we read *Anne of Green Gables* and the Books to one another in cable-knit sweaters by the fireplace, and that one of these evenings he took my hand and placed on my finger a garnet with two small pearls on the side, after which we embarked upon writerly lives modeled after Joan Didion and John Gregory Dunne.

For my story, the story of *My Life as Kelly Kathleen Ferguson*, this was the ending I craved, and maybe I even deserved it. After years of dithering, I had gathered up the courage to pursue my life dreams. I had worked hard. I had sacrificed. I was of a certain age. I was ready for the happy golden ending where the handsome but aloof man melts for our intrepid heroine with the heart of gold.

Sounds nice, doesn't it?

Except that's not what happened.

I came to discover, like Laura, that a commitment to forward direction is not without unforeseen consequences.

Soon after their marriage, Almanzo and Laura suffered the reality that their western pioneer dream was not going to happen. Year after year the Wilders tried to raise a wheat crop only to be foiled by the Dakota climate. Everything I know about Laura and Almanzo tells me they pulled out the stops. They took out loans, woke up an hour earlier and went to bed an hour later, sacrificing their honeymoon years for the sake of establishing a future, to no avail. Their house burned down. They contracted illnesses. Worst of all, they lost an infant son.

The First Four Years was discovered in Laura's desk after her death and published posthumously, which could explain why it has the pallor of the undead. Different theories exist as to why *The First Four Years*, aside from being incredibly depressing, isn't, if I may speak plainly, very good. If nothing else, the book serves as a cautionary tale against publishing unfinished work. Dr. Buzzkill claims that without Rose "running it through her typewriter," Laura wasn't capable of writing a fully fleshed-out book on her own. An alternate theory, proposed by Pamela Smith Hill, is that *Four Years* was Laura's attempt at a book targeting an adult audience, so she adopted a more somber tone. Roger Lea McBride (whom Rose named heir to the Wilder intellectual property) writes in the introduction that he believed after Almanzo died, Laura lost interest in revising.

I have another idea.

We can talk about depression and malaise and ennui or whatever else we want to call it, but the classic diagnosis would be heartbreak.

At this time change was in the air again. My lease ran out in a month, my teaching position was coming to an end and local employment opportunities ran scarce. I could tell that I might get stuck again if I wasn't careful. More than anything, I feared stagnation.

My Manly and I made grand plans. For the following year he would live in Prince Edward Island, stroll red sand beaches and contemplate the greenness of gables, while I would move to New Orleans, wear antique slips and sip mint juleps on French Quarter balconies. Once established in these terribly romantic locales, My Manly and I would visit one another. PEI and New Orleans. Acadians and Cajuns. Mussels and gulf oysters. The seafood and the writing would be terrific. Anne Shirley and Laura Ingalls sat on my desk side-by-side. After this year, we would see. I admit I was hoping we would return to Montana, the place of my pioneer heart, and forge a life of letters to the backdrop of a smack-you-upside-the-face, jaw-droppingly inspirational landscape. For now, though, it seemed imperative that I not sit around and wait.

I set to the tasks of downsizing and packing, but I had to flog myself along. This move wasn't inspired by the same excitement as my trek out West. New Orleans was, truthfully, a half-baked destination, fueled by one friend I knew, some vague concept of my "southern return" and a Jazz Fest weekend from my freshman year of college—a murky recollection at best. But I'd learned that I couldn't afford to stop and ask myself too many questions or the ruminations would paralyze me. I boxed and purged like a robot until the day came when my bed and sofa were gone. After the brief excitement of lifting these giant furnishings out the back stairs, my apartment was silent and empty. I sat on the wood floors with the exposed dust bunnies for company and sneezed. My Manly had already left for PEI, and I began to wonder why I was here dealing with all of this alone. I found myself slipping back into "what if" mode. *What if I'm making a terrible mistake?*

When in doubt, go for tacos.

My local Mexican refuge was up the road from my apartment. The plan was to stroll up, grab some lunch and consider my options afterwards. I was just about there, when I saw a couple headed toward me down Higgins Street. It took me a minute to focus in my exhausted packing haze before I recognized Joe and Greta from My Manly's photos. I had never met Joe and Greta, but My Manly had talked about them so much I felt as if I knew them. Joe and Greta. Joe and Greta. Joe and Greta. My understanding was that they had moved East, but obviously they had returned. What to do? Should I stop? Or pretend I didn't see them? We wound up standing in line together, but as Joe and Greta's pupils remained undilated, I could tell they didn't recognize me. I could choose to be anonymous. My hair hung in greasy strands from packing and cleaning. I was dressed in a stained, stretched wifebeater paired with flappy chinos sporting a giant crotch hole.

Probably ignoring them was best, I thought. *I should just walk in, get my taco, and when I got home I would call My Manly and—*

"Hi, I'm Kelly," I blurted. Joe and Greta reacted with expressions blank as Willie Oleson's school slate. Instant, hot regret flushed through my body. Greta's wide, catlike face studied me. Conclusion: Not impressed. Joe was handsome in a square-jawed, graphic novel hero way. A giant thought bubble loomed over his head that read, "Uhhhhhhhh."

"I am Manly's, er, friend," I stumbled on, noticing that I had dropped the prefix *girl*.

"What do you know," Greta said, as she looked past me, in vain hope of a helicopter to airlift her away. "We were just saying Missoula is the kind of place you run into people."

I formed the apex of an acute triangle of acute silence. Painfully awkward small talk ensued, and the truth dawned on me—these people had no idea who I was. That, or what they had heard was not good.

"Well!" I said.

"...," Joe said.

"Yeah," Greta limped on. "Joe and I are staying at Manly's place until he gets back from Prince Edward Island next month."

Next month?

I don't know what anyone said after that because the world went swimmy. That I didn't know that Joe and Greta were staying in My Manly's apartment was the first shockwave, but that was nothing compared to the realization that My Manly had been lying to me about his plans for weeks, months even. He wasn't moving to PEI for a year to embark upon a spiritual inner journey, he was *vacationing*.

It occurred to me that he had lied to me because otherwise, I might not have followed through on my plans to move.

My Manly wasn't suffering from Male Commitment Freak-Out Syndrome. "It" wasn't complicated. He hadn't ingested a poison doughnut. Jupiter's moons were fine. The waxing. The waning. All of it. Maybe he did or maybe he didn't know what love felt like, or what was wrong with him, but he knew what he wanted.

He wanted out.

I stood in utter silence, unable to speak. Joe and Greta decided maybe they weren't so hungry for tacos after all. They were shadows in the doorway for a moment, before Greta went on tiptoe, whispered in Joe's ear, and they both skiddooed. I gazed at their absence, the door framing a white rectangle of sun for a moment before I collapsed. I'd like to thank the kind person, whoever and wherever you may be, who picked up my tab, gently guided me to the self-serve soda and handed me a few brown paper napkins so I could blow my nose.

Of course, no one ever dumps you "all of a sudden." What "all of a sudden" means is your willful ignorance of the situation. There was a reason that I was getting rid of all my belongings instead of putting them into storage.

Deep down, I knew I wasn't coming back.

Deep down, I knew that My Manly wasn't My Manly, but Just Another Manly.

Deep down, I knew that in this romantic drama, my tragic flaw of optimism had clouded my judgment about what I had.

Metaphorically speaking, I had been trying to farm the Great American Desert, and like Pa, one plague of locusts wasn't enough for me. No, I had to plant another big ole' wheat crop and build a house on credit. Then the locusts returned and there I was, broke and forced to wander off in search of work in old, holey boots.

When treasures don't mean anything, they become trinkets. The china shepherdess. The fiddle. Carrie's china dog. These items had meaning because of the relationships they represented. I imagine if Pa had left Ma for a dental hygienist she would have taken those carved brackets from that Big Woods Christmas and split them with an axe. I amassed the sparkle flask, the Barclay II supper club dinner napkin, the rose petals, the Valentine box, the key to Room 241 at the Sip 'n' Dip Lounge et. al. and prepared for burial by dumpster.

I was grooving right along, purging like a champ. The Easter basket. Maneki Neko cat. His L.L. Bean flannel shirt.

Then—

—Anne Shirley in eight volumes.

I'm funny about books. You may have noticed. I didn't have a childhood connection to Green Gables, so technically I wasn't obligated, but I knew that Anne Shirley meant to others what Laura meant to me. My friend Anna, for one, had grown up a Gables girl. It could be I was still clinging to a desperate hope and that I was messed up and needed (even more?) therapy. I didn't know what to do, but I knew I couldn't throw away those books.

I packed the green box set.

There was nothing to do but go on. I tried to get in the spirit of my new adventure, but when I crossed the Montana state line, knowing I might never return, a sharp pain spliced my chest. The hailstorm in Wyoming and tornado in Nebraska did nothing to improve my disposition. I won't drone on about poor, poor me, but dumped and alone and bankrupt and unemployed and driving for twelve hours a stretch in the summer heat—this was not great.

I was backtrailing.

Somewhere along some interstate, Mr. Turtle "slipped" into the side compartment of my car, and I left him there.

I washed up in New Orleans a limp, wet rag of a human being with a skillet and twenty boxes of books. Through a cash advance on my credit card, I took an apartment in the Lower Garden District, two rooms carved out of a giant, pink Greek Revival house. The place was small but had high ceilings and a little courtyard. A futon and a large, oak antique desk had been left behind, and I unpacked and piled my books against a wall.

I had made a promise to myself that I would write, and for my first project, I would write about the woman who had made me want to be a writer. By this point, I had conceived the beginnings of this book and worked up a few chapter drafts. An idea that had initially seemed like a one-way hike up Crazy Mountain began to take on the shape of reality. Ending Number One (true love) had failed, but maybe I could pull out Ending Number Two: Our intrepid heroine with the heart of gold moves to New Orleans, writes a best-selling book and triumphs.

The only problem was that as obsessively as I had wanted to write about Laura, I found I had nothing to say about Laura. I would get up, open my laptop, sit at the oak desk and stare out the long window protected by scrolled, iron bars. When the afternoon heat blared, I gave up even trying to pretend, lay on the floor and rasped in short breaths. Perhaps moving to post-Katrina New Orleans was the perfect idea—a damaged woman rebuilding alongside a damaged city—or maybe timing my arrival with hurricane season wasn't such a great idea. The air was hot and oppressive. People were nervous.

To be clear, I didn't like that being dumped had put me in a catatonic state, any more than I appreciated the cliché of an impending fortieth birthday getting me down. I tried little pep talks—*C'mon, intrepid heroine!* But all my attempts at reasoning or cajoling or even outright yelling failed. I had coded. Whatever had been driving me had snuck out in the middle of the night.

Ultimately, I learned that feeling can be divorced from action. I put the Books on my desk and the map I had purchased from Carrie and Grace in Mansfield on my wall. Through sheer force of will I managed to eke out a bit of progress each day. I had no idea how one went about writing a book, or then how one got this book published once completed. I bought a bunch of how-to books that involved a great deal of exclamation points and figured out the situation the best I could. For those wondering, here's the skinny: for nonfiction you write a proposal and try to land an agent. So that's what I set out to do. Maybe some people "whip up" book proposals, but apparently I wasn't wired that way. It took me a solid month to figure out how I should word the first sentence to my query letter. I knew that as a complete unknown my proposal *might* get a glimpse before it was sorted out. I read that the average agent gets about fifty query letters a day. How could I, Ms. Nobody, get someone to pay attention?

I eventually reached the point where there was nothing more to do beyond going to the French Quarter and purchasing a few voodoo charms. I was terrified to send my proposal out because I wasn't sure I could handle rejection, not in this state of mind, but I steeled myself and threw my dream into the slush pile. I targeted my ideal agency, a big New York agency that represented a stable of famous nonfiction writers I admired.

Guess what?

Three weeks later an agent contacted me. The agent had even dressed as Laura Ingalls for Halloween. She thought my book was a terrific idea, and she loved my material. We began brainstorming ideas, and I could feel the New York publishing machine shifting into high gear, which was scary, but also thrilling.

I don't know if you have spent your entire life waiting for something exciting and great to happen, but as a lifelong, avid reader of children's literature, I pretty much had. I had been insane to go in debt based on the belief that I could be a best-selling writer, and it was insane to send my proposal to only one agency thinking this would work. I was of the age where I should buckle down, make compromises and contribute to my 401K, not gamble with my life— but then, here I was, the star of my own *Lifetime* movie. The intrepid heroine with the heart of gold had kicked ass.

But guess what again?

It turned out that just a month earlier, another writer had sold a humorous nonfiction book about Laura Ingalls Wilder, in which she proposed writing about a trip where she retraced her childhood heroine's pioneer journey.

Kind of like the trip I already took.

The agent told me my project was dead, apologized and advised me to move on.

The end.

What?

The truth was, that while I had made all these grand declarations about the joys of risking and personal growth, I had no intention of being one of those people who scratches off their lottery ticket only to see, "try again." No, I had, without even realizing how much, counted on my life functioning as a narrative. Certain obstacles were to be expected. These were the twists and turns that made any story worthwhile until the ending, the real ending, the "happy golden" ending, worked out. But now I had lost faith in overcoming obstacles. All I could believe was that after all this moving, driving and striving, I had traveled in one giant, transcontinental circle.

This time, there was a kicker.

Laura.

I felt betrayed. "Signs." Right. Losing my boyfriend was bad. Losing the agency contract was bad. But that was nothing compared to losing Laura. A childhood Barbie, dressed in a calico prairie outfit purchased in Walnut Grove, was falling out of one of my semi-unpacked boxes. When I saw this doll, it struck me that trying to forge an adult life based on a childhood talisman was incredibly naive.

The souvenirs of my trip had brought me a silly, quiet joy. They had been sitting on my desk to keep me company as I worked. Now, like all of My Manly's presents, the Laura stuff represented the absurd hopes of an immature woman ruled by superstition. Even the name *Laura* became a thorn every time I heard it. *Laura* is a popular name, I learned. A box of Laura stuff had made the cross-country move cut, but I wanted the reminders of my past, foolish self out of sight. I got to work purging. I was cruising right along, tossing like a champ. The covered wagon refrigerator magnets. The bookmarks. The bonnets.

Then—

—Laura Ingalls Wilder in nine volumes.

I could not face this right now, not without cracking entirely.

I packed the Books back up.

Laura Ingalls, you remember Anne Shirley.

All my life, in times of great loneliness and personal peril, I had turned to the Books, crawled in bed and read.

These days I just crawled in bed.

Weeks passed like this—days staring out the window, nights chasing cockroaches with a shoe—until one morning I woke up with one solution to one problem. A start. I drove up St. Charles to the Uptown library, a huge, old mansion on a hill, recently reopened post-Katrina. I climbed the cracked, concrete temple steps with my offering. The circulation desk was in the foyer, in front of a giant, restored wooden mantle.

"Oooh!" gushed the young librarian, when I handed over the green box. "We have one set but could use another, and we were missing *Rilla of Ingleside*. I know a girl who is going to be so excited to see this. Oh God, I remember knowing exactly how Anne felt about those puffed sleeves."

I knew what it was to be a southern girl, drenched in sweat, dreaming of cooler climes. I wondered if the librarian was aware of hugging the box set to her chest.

I wished Anne Shirley the best and said my good-byes.

That I had come up with such a perfect solution to the Green Gables predicament cheered me up. Back in the car, my eye caught a glimpse of shiny green. It was Mr. Turtle, who had remained in the side door compartment all this time. A sudden, sharp remorse for having ditched him pinched my heart. He was undamaged, except for a small watermark on his chest, which gave me a pang of guilt. I brushed off Mr. Turtle and placed him in my palm, staring one more time into the two beads stitched firmly on either side of his head. Like Jack the faithful bulldog, he had been my loyal traveling companion through miles of lonesome prairie. I put him back on the dash.

With these reconciliations, there was nothing to do but face Laura again. I was pretty much over sitting at my desk and staring out the window, so I took off walking down St. Charles. The sky was blue-gray, a spooky wind whipping through the streets. A nervous energy simmered, warm air blaring the first rumble of storm season. The secret about hurricane season is that although you are supposed to be panicked and working on your evacuation plan, you don't want to go anywhere because the wind feels terrific and the ion charge electrifies.

I waved at the daiquiri store posse and moved past the Lower Garden into the quieter business district. I walked by new restaurants and residences that had taken down the boarded-up windows and reopened. I passed buildings that didn't look any different from

Katrina day-after footage, even though it had been four years since the storm. Moving past the banks and hotels, I cut across palm-tree-lined Canal Street and plunged into the Quarter. I took in one block of Bourbon Street with no need to linger, soon craving relief from the loud, pulsing desperation of karaoke bars and plastic beads months out of date. I appreciated the irony that only a few blocks over from the Huge Ass Beer stand was the house where William Faulkner had written his first novel. That so many revered authors— Eudora Welty, Walker Percy, Robert Penn Warren—had worked in New Orleans was inspiring, but also intimidating. Supposedly my life had been building to this big dream of being a writer, but I wasn't sure anymore. It could be that I still wanted to write, just not about Laura. I had no idea. As a hollow person, I didn't know what I thought about anything anymore, but I couldn't do nothing forever.

I didn't like what I was going to have to face.

I had been avoiding this moment, preferring to sit and stare.

Was my love for Laura superficial in that I loved her only so long as she gave me what I wanted? The truth was that I had been wrong to blame Laura because I didn't get my happy golden ending. Because Laura's story had never, ever been that if I kept trying everything would work out the way I wanted. In fact, if Laura had taught me anything, it was that life often didn't turn out the way you planned. Disaster and disappointment strike. All the time. Laura chronicled her hardships. She contracted diseases—scarlet fever, malaria and diphtheria. Her sister went blind. She survived blizzards in a shack. Crops failed. She went hungry. She met and married her true love only to suffer an onslaught of disaster. Over the course of her lifetime, Laura moved ten times, each time paring down to the barest of the bare and starting over. The Books might read now as if they were born, but I knew otherwise, that Laura had struggled with multiple drafts before publishing the classics we know today.

Not for one second did I wish I had stayed on that front porch in Durham.

I gulped.

It couldn't be helped.

I didn't know what I should do, but I knew what Laura would do.

I went home and unpacked the yellow box set.

SELECTED BIBLIOGRAPHY

Anderson, William. *Laura Ingalls Wilder: A Biography.* New York:
Harper Trophy, 1992.

Baum, Frank L. *The Wizard of Oz.* New York: Signet Classics,
2006.

Bettmann, Otto. *The Good Old Days: They Were Terrible!* New York:
Random House, 1974.

Blunt, Judy. *Breaking Clean.* New York: Random House, 2002.

Capote, Truman. *In Cold Blood.* New York: Random House, 1962.

Frazier, Ian. *Great Plains.* New York: Picador, 2001.

Frontier House. PBS, WETA, Arlington, Virginia/WNET, New
York, 2002.

Forrest, Steven. *The Inner Sky: The Dynamic New Astrology for
Everyone.* San Diego: ACS Publications, 1989.

Hill, Pamela Smith. *Laura Ingalls Wilder: A Writer's Life.* South
Dakota Biography Series. Pierre: South Dakota State Historical
Society, 2007.

Hines, Stephen W. (ed.). *Laura Ingalls Wilder, Farm Journalist.*
Columbia: University of Missouri Press, 2007.

Holtz, William. *The Ghost in the Little House: The Life of Rose Wilder
Lane.* Missouri Biography Series. Columbia: University of
Missouri Press, 1993.

Keillor, Garrison. *Life Among the Lutherans.* Minneapolis: Augsburg
Books, 2009.

Krakauer, Jon. *Into the Wild.* New York: Anchor Books, 1997.

Laskin, David. *The Children's Blizzard.* New York: Harper Collins,
2004.

London, Jack. *The Call of the Wild.* New York: Book of the
Month Club, 2000.

Marquart, Debra. *The Horizontal World: Growing Up Wild in the
Middle of Nowhere.* New York: Counterpoint, 2006.

Miller, John. *Becoming Laura Ingalls Wilder: The Woman Behind the Legend*. Missouri Biography Series. Columbia: University of Missouri Press, 1998.

Stanley, Alessandra. "A Nostalgic Roundup to Happy Trails." *New York Times*, July 30, 2003.

Strasser, Susan. *Never Done: A History of American Housework*. New York: Pantheon, 1982.

Stratton, Joanna L. *Pioneer Women: Voices from the Kansas Frontier*. New York: Simon and Schuster, 1981.

Werner, Emmy. *Pioneer Children on the Journey West*. Boulder: Westview Press, 1995.

West, Elliot. *Growing Up with the Country: Children on the Western Frontier*. Albuquerque: University of New Mexico Press, 1989.

ACKNOWLEDGMENTS

Thanks to my family.

Thanks to Kevin Morgan Watson and Press 53 for believing in this book.

Thanks to Robin Miura, for her editorial guidance and support this past year.

Thanks to the University of Montana and former President Dennison, who when I asked for a travel grant so that I could traipse around the Midwest in a Laura dress, said yes.

Thanks to my Montana and Ohio nonfictionistas who read fledgling drafts along the way. Your voices are with me.

Laura always had great friends, and so have I. I only mention Anna Mueller Luce (Annnaaaaa!) by name in this memoir, but in truth, there's a village of Annas supporting me. You all cared about this book when I could not. A special shout-out to Claire Guyton, who might have tracked me down and put the hurt on if I didn't finish.

Thanks to Renita Remasco and Laurel Wamsley for their thoughtful comments on my first completed draft. And thanks to Trina Burke for early editorial help.

Thanks, Catherine Chamis, for the map, and everything.

Thanks to Doug Karger.

Finally, I extend gratitude to my Rose Wilder Lanes (editors/ mentors), who have shaped me as a writer these past four years: Judy Blunt, Bryan Di Salvatore, Kevin Canty, Deidre McNamer and Dinty W. Moore.

KELLY KATHLEEN FERGUSON's work has appeared in *mental_floss magazine*, *Poets & Writers*, the *Gettysburg Review* (for which she received a Pushcart nomination), *McSweeney's Internet Tendency*, and *Brevity*, among other publications. She has an MFA from the University of Montana, and is currently working on a PhD in creative nonfiction at Ohio University. Kelly is Libra, Cancer rising, moon in Aquarius. She is Irish/French/German, lapsed Roman Catholic, and right-brained. Kelly once received a minority scholarship for a machinist certification program at Durham Technical Community College. When Kelly was four, she ate a mothball and had to have her stomach pumped, or she would have died.

CPSIA information can be obtained at www.ICGtesting.com
Printed in the USA
BVOW041117130712

R4635200001B/R46352PG294922BVX1B/1/P